D1430956

Indians of the
pacific northwest

INDIANS
of the
PACIFIC
NORTHWEST

From the Coming of the White Man
to the Present Day

Vine Deloria, Jr.

DOUBLEDAY & COMPANY, INC. GARDEN CITY, NEW YORK

PHOTO CREDITS

Andrew T. Kelley, courtesy: Smithsonian Institution National Anthropological Archives, Bureau of American Ethnology Collection, pp. 30, 31, 158

Smithsonian Institution National Anthropological Archives, Bureau of American Ethnology Collection, pp. 24, 27, 91

University of Washington, Special Collections, Seattle, pp. 72, 73, 75, 76, 79, 80, 83, 93, 94, 98

Dolores Varela, pp. 167, 168, 170, 173, 175

Library of Congress Cataloging in Publication Data

Deloria, Vine.
    Indians of the Pacific Northwest.

    Includes index.
    SUMMARY: A history of the tribes of the Pacific Northwest from the coming of the white man to the present day.
    1. Indians of North America—Northwest, Pacific—Juvenile literature. 2. Indians of North America—Nothwest, Pacific—Government relations—Juvenile literature. [1. Indians of North America—Northwest, Pacific. 2. Indians of North America—Northwest, Pacific—Government relations] I. Title.
E78.N77D44   979.5'004'97
        Library of Congress Catalog Card Number 74–18789
        ISBN 0-385-09790-5 Trade
             0-385-09791-3 Prebound

Indians of the
pacific northwest

chapter

ONE

WHEN I was first elected to the directorship of the National
Congress of American Indians, I was introduced to the tribes
of the Pacific Northwest, particularly those tribes that live in
and around the Puget Sound area. The Makahs, who live on
Cape Flattery, one of the northern peninsulas of Washington
State, told me how a Spanish expedition in the late 1700s had
invaded their lands and built a fort. The Makahs bided their
time, cleverly captured the fort one morning, and sent the
Spanish fleeing for their boats leaving behind cannons, guns,
and all manner of goods. While the name of Juan de Fuca
was given to the strait between the lands of the Makahs and
Vancouver Island, the lands and waters remained in the
hands of the Indians for some time afterward.

The chief complaint of the Indians of the Pacific Northwest when they would come to the national Indian political
conventions would be that the whites, particularly the of-

ficials of the fish and game departments of Washington State, were violating their treaties and harassing the Indian fishermen. I grew up in South Dakota, a member of the Sioux tribe, and when we talked about fish in that country we were talking about something approximately six inches long that you were sometimes lucky to get out of a creek in mid-summer. So I could never figure out just what the problem was in Washington State, and the idea of people complaining because they couldn't go fishing seemed a little absurd to me at the time.

But the coastal tribes kept after the rest of us. They would compare the salmon with the buffalo, telling us how the salmon was to them what the buffalo had been to the Plains tribes. It was, we all agreed, ridiculous to compare a tiny fish with the magnificent animal that had provided us with food, clothing, weapons, and other articles of our culture. We were polite but firm and tried to press on to larger and more important topics of discussion that affected Indians all over the nation.

Finally, perhaps in some despair over the stupidity of this Plains Indian they were trying to educate, the Pacific Northwest tribes invited me to come to Washington State and attend a meeting on Indian problems. I was eager to get out and meet the people of the different tribes, and so I accepted and flew to Seattle. A car picked me up and we went to the state capital, Olympia, where the Indians were having a banquet with their congressman, Lloyd Meeds, who has spent his time in Congress working hard with the tribes to resolve some of their problems.

There were nearly fifty Indians at the banquet, and, of course, salmon was served. Everyone ate his fill of the delicious meal, and after the ceremonies and speeches one of the Indians took me to the kitchen to see the remains of the sal-

8

mon that had provided us with our meal. I was confronted with the skeletal remains of a gigantic fish, far surpassing in size the tiny catfish of my youth. When I learned that this one salmon had fed the entire banquet, I came to understand why the salmon was so important to these people.

Over the next decade I kept in close touch with the tribes of the Puget Sound area and came to know many of their leaders very well, as friends and as fellow workers. They were always courteous, hospitable, and generous, often sending me smoked salmon when their delegations came East. I developed a special admiration for the tribes because they had persevered against incredible odds over the past century and were quite often betrayed by the federal officials who were supposed to help them.

I found that the more I learned about the people of the Pacific Northwest and their history the more I wanted to learn. In 1970 I moved to upper Puget Sound to teach at Western Washington State College, in Bellingham, which was a mere twelve miles from the Lummi reservation. In the year and a half that I lived in the Northwest, only a half mile from the reservation, I learned much more about the tribes of the area. It always puzzled me that so little was known about these exciting people, who had developed a very sophisticated fishing technology centuries before the coming of the white man and who had successfully maintained their fishing culture even a century after they had been overwhelmed by the settlers.

To my knowledge, no adequate history of these tribes has ever been written. Most studies on Indian life in the Pacific Northwest have concentrated on the tribes farther north, in British Columbia, such as the Kwakiutl and the Nootka. These tribes, who live in what is now Canada, had a ceremony known as the "potlatch," in which they gave away immense amounts of goods as a means of determining their social status and wealth, somewhat in the same manner as the very rich in today's society tend to create foundations to distribute their wealth. This Indian practice fascinated the early scholars who visited the area, and they tended to overemphasize the custom in their scholarly works, completely overlooking the other facets of Indian life that made the people of the area so interesting. Today when you look at a book on the Indians of the Pacific Northwest, chances are that you will find a great deal on the Kwakiutl and the Nootka but very little on the Lummi, the Makah, the Skagit, or the Nooksack, and certainly only the slightest mention of the Chehalis, the Nisqually, or the Chinook. Yet these tribes have a history well worth learning.

It is perhaps best to start with a description of their lands, for the manner in which these different tribes adapted to their lands pretty much determined how their social and political customs, and certainly their great economic wealth, came about. So we will concentrate on the area from the Canadian border along the west side of the Cascade mountain range, down to the Columbia River, and south of that river a little way into the Willamette Valley.

The Cascades form a giant barrier on the West Coast, catching the rains and winds from the Pacific, which blow constantly inland. In prehistoric times the volcanoes of the Cascade were active, and some of the larger ones still smoke. Mt. Baker, the largest of the far-northern mountains, formed part of the eastern border of the area, and within sight of its large snow field lived the Lummi, Nooksack, Samish, and Semiahmoo around the Bellingham Bay area. To the south lived the Skagits, Swinomish, and Snohomish, near Whidbey Island and the Skagit Valley flood plains.

The Seattle area was settled by a number of small villages of Indians who fished the Green, White, Puyallup, and Nisqually rivers, and from that multitude of villages have come the Duwamish, Nisqually, Puyallup, and other tribes of today. The Nisqually ranged around the southern end of Puget Sound, near present-day Tacoma and Olympia. Beside them on the west, extending on around the western shore of Puget Sound, were the Squaxins and the Suquamish. On Cape Flattery lived the Makahs, and south of them along the coast were the Hohs, the Quileutes, the Queets, the Quinaults, and finally, along the Oregon coasts, the Chinooks.

Separating the lands of the coast tribes from the lands of the Puget Sound tribes were the majestic Olympic Mountains and the giant rain forest that blankets their slopes. Mt. Rainier and other high mountains had their own glaciers and snow fields, which, along with the rain forests, ensured that the whole area west of the Cascades was interlaced with rivers, streams, and creeks of all sizes, fed in the fall and winter by the incessant rains from the ocean and in the summer by the melting of the snows. The White River, for example, was so called because of the color of the water as it came down the slopes of Mt. Rainier. Other rivers seemed to change color as the seasons changed and the water shifted from melted snow to seasonal rain and back again.

Most of the mountains had special names given to them by the Indians who lived near them. Mt. Rainier, for example, which figured prominently in their folklore, was called Dahkobeed by the Duwamish, Tacobud by the Nisqually, and Takkobad by the Puyallups. The Lummi name for Mt. Baker, Komo Kulshan, meant the great white watcher; the mountain was said to watch over the people. Some of the Indian stories seemed ridiculous to the early settlers, especially those that accounted for the earliest geologic changes, but modern discoveries bear out the story line of the old Indian legends very well.

One old story told of the days when the eastern part of Washington was a gigantic lake and there was no Columbia River. The coyote, who was generally helpful to the people, realized that if there was no river the salmon could not come up into the lake and the people would starve. So he made a hole in the mountains, and water began to drain from the lake into the ocean, forming the Columbia. Soon the salmon came and the people were fed. For a while a stone bridge existed where the coyote had dug through the Cascades, and people could cross the Columbia on this bridge. But eventually, during an earthquake, the bridge collapsed, forming the cascades of the Columbia, and the people had to use boats to cross the river. The funny thing is that new mapping techniques via satellite seem to indicate that a large lake did once exist in eastern Washington and that a channel eventually was formed which is now the Columbia River.

So completely did the rivers dominate the region that there were practically no trails through the dense forests at all. The Indians all traveled on the rivers, and except for the tribes that lived far inland on the slopes of the mountains (called "horse" Indians by the water peoples), everyone lived by the water and used canoes to get around. As the rivers were so important, it was natural that the people would keep track of each other according to river systems or drainages. The suffix "-amish," which is found on many of the tribal names, for example Swinomish, Stilaguamish, Snohomish, Suquamish, Duwamish, and others, indicates that they are the "people of" a certain river system.

The Puget Sound area was one of the most heavily populated areas north of Mexico City before the coming of the white man. There was no formal tribal organization among the different groups, as was the case farther east and south. The rigid social system of the Pueblo villages, for example, and the highly developed clan system of the Iroquois were entirely foreign to this land. Rather, the people lived almost everywhere in very small groups. The average village consisted of one and perhaps as many as three long houses, comfortably containing from four to six families. They were usually constructed at river junctions or along favorite fishing sites such as a falls, or cascade, of a river.

The unusual aspect of Puget Sound life was that most of the villages had both summer houses, which were comparable to modern summer cabins, and winter houses at the more settled village from which the people generally took their name. Winter, though dreary and very rainy, was the time for the most important religious ceremonies, with the one exception of the first-salmon ceremony, observed at the beginning of the salmon runs, in spring. When not involved in their religious rituals, the Indians spent their time making needed household goods and fishing. The steelhead trout, which returns to the streams in winter, provided them with fresh meat, and food preserved during the previous summer further supplemented their diet.

Spring, summer, and early fall were devoted to fishing, gathering berries, and preparing for the winter. Many families wandered far over the islands that dotted Puget Sound and the upper-straits waters. The Lummis scattered all over the San Juan Islands in their reef-netting activities, the Makahs went far out to sea to hunt whales, and other tribes spread throughout the region in search of berries, camas roots, and other delicacies of the table. In the summertime there were many large gatherings of people from the various villages. It

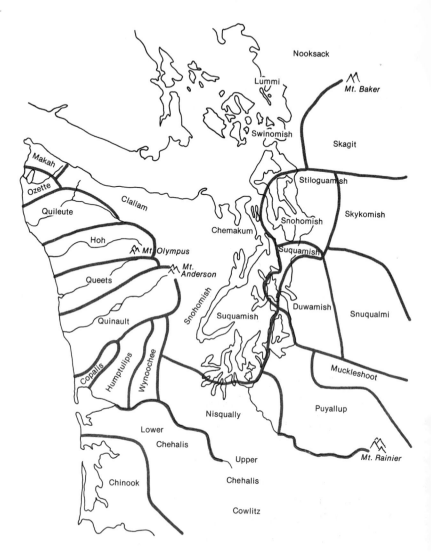

The traditional lands of the tribes of western Washington prior to the arrival of the white man.

was a time for large feasts and visiting. Marriages were arranged and business transacted between families of different villages. Summer for the Indians resembled vacation time today in the Pacific Northwest. Everyone tried to get away to a quiet place to relax and engage in frequent celebrations.

This comparison between modern life and the life of the Indians before the coming of the white man is more than apt. One might have characterized the region as being completely suburbanized during the summer because of the variety of fishing sites used by the different families. Fishing stations were hereditary, for the most part, and some tribes appeared to specialize in the catching and preparation of certain species of salmon while others concentrated their efforts on another species. People would even share the lengths of streams, and so sophisticated was their taste that many said they could tell, from one bite of the food, exactly what stream a fish had come from and which group of Indians had prepared it.

Depending upon the type of salmon caught and the weather conditions prevailing, salmon could be prepared in any number of ways. Sometimes it was smoked, other times, with a good dry wind, it was cured by wind-drying. Sun-drying was risky because of the high humidity. The salmon eggs, considered a great winter delicacy, were also dried and smoked.

Fish was not the only food of the people, although it certainly was the major item on the menu. The larger land animals—deer, elk, and bear—were very important. These animals tended to live on the many small prairies and foothills of the Cascades. All the tribes hunted them, particularly in the wintertime. An extensive trade between the inland people and the coastal tribes, extending sometimes across the Cascades to the eastern part of Washington, was based on the exchange of dried or smoked salmon for buffalo, antelope, and other meat delicacies.

Mountain-goat meat was considered a treat among many of the tribes, and they were happy to trade their fish for it. Strangely enough, the absolutely best salmon was considered to be that of the Yakimas, who lived across the Cascades on the Columbia. The Puget Sound people, who had more salmon than they knew what to do with, often traveled across the snowy Cascades to trade for salmon that had come up the Columbia to the famous Celilo Falls of the Yakimas. Celilo Falls, unfortunately, is no more. After the Second World War, dams for generating electrical power were built on the Columbia, and the famous fishing site was flooded.

The women and girls gathered shellfish such as clams, oysters, and crabs, the best crabs, of course, being those of Dungeness Bay, which was in the land of the Clallams. They also gathered the camas root, similar to a potato, and a seemingly infinite variety of berries. Years after white settlement, Indian women had at their disposal over two hundred recipes for preparing and combining food staples such as salmon, berries, and camas roots and other vegetables.

With such a taste for delicacies it was no wonder that the peoples of the Puget Sound area developed a very extensive trading system. With five species of salmon alone, oil from seals, whales, and dogfish, and a variety of other fish and foods, the trading for various commodities became quite complicated.

The sockeye salmon, for example, did not run in any of the streams on the Strait of Juan de Fuca, the area where the Makahs and the Clallams lived. But it did run on the western coast, south of Cape Flattery, in the Ozette River. Thus trade

16

for sockeye developed. The Makahs did not have sufficient cedar of suitable quality for either houses or canoes, so they traded with the Nootkas on Vancouver Island for cedar canoes and planks. What did they use for trading purposes? Whale and seal oil, dried herring roe, which formed a type of caviar, and other products that could be obtained only in the Pacific Ocean and required very large canoes made only by the Nootkas!

The western Indians sold slaves (people they had captured in war), haikwa (a precious sea shell), dried clams, and camas roots to the tribes in the mountains and farther inland in exchange for mountain-sheep wool, porcupine quills, embroidery, and particularly for a certain kind of grass from which they made delicate threads for sewing. The peoples who lived on the western slopes of the Cascades brought mountain-goat meat to the Makahs and traded it for whale meat and oil. The Makahs, in turn, traded the meat for red ochre, used for paint and cosmetics, and found only in Quileute territory. When one considers the complex number of trades among tribal groups in the days before the white man came, then it is possible to understand how the Indians of the area welcomed the fur traders, the first non-Indians to come among them.

One can also understand how the hostility between the Indians and the later settlers arose. The people who followed the traders and trappers were primarily farmers, who did not enjoy a trade fair and the endless dickering for bargains that always accompanied trading. For the Indian, trade, besides being profitable, was just plain fun, and provided an exciting opportunity to visit other peoples. Because the food and other trade items were so plentiful, people had to become specialists in order to produce goods for trade. One could not simply smoke salmon because everyone did. Rather, the different villages had to develop speciality items that would be coveted by other tribes in order to participate in the trade. So no one grew very rich and no one was very poor. It was a system that worked out well for all.

chapter
TWO

T HE picture of a native paradise in the Pacific Northwest is not the whole story, however, and one only begins to learn of the complexity of pre-Columbian Indian life with an understanding of Indian technology. Unfortunately, except for a few scholarly studies on Indian house-building and fishing techniques (the latter based on a system of twig fences, called "weirs," scattered throughout the streams), there has been little investigation of the real technology by which the Puget Sound Indians gained their livelihood.

Imagine, if you will, being placed in a land where a great variety of salmon filled each and every river, where ducks and geese filled the evening sky, where berries literally dripped from the bushes at harvest time, and where crabs, clams, mussels, and oysters abounded. One's first inclination would be to fish, hunt, and gather as much food as possible, but the real question would be *how* to gather this food as efficiently as possible and how to preserve it. In developing techniques for catching fish, preserving berries, and cooking shellfish, the Indians of the area were supreme. In order to understand the development of Indian skills, let us examine the great variety of techniques they used to gather food and imagine ourselves carefully observing the clever use of every resource in hunting and fishing.

First, there were at least five different kinds of fishing, distinguished by the nature of the water in which the fish lived. There were freshwater lakes; freshwater streams and creeks that drained into the various inlets and bays on the sound and the straits; the waters of the shallow bays and estuaries, basically the tideland flats; the inlets and the sound itself, which were considerably deeper and broader bodies of water than the shallow bays; and finally there were the ocean and the large straits, virtually boundless in length and depth.

Shellfish such as clams and oysters could be collected in the shallow bays and on the beaches. At the appropriate times the women and girls of the villages turned out to harvest these shellfish, drying some of them for the winter but generally preparing a gigantic feast of fresh clams or oysters. Crabs were harvested in the same way, but these shellfish tended to be concentrated along the northern end of the Olympic Peninsula. Crabs were usually plentiful in the spring and were difficult to preserve, so they provided only a seasonal treat.

Salmon-fishing techniques varied greatly, according to the nature of the water system. On freshwater lakes, the object would be to catch the fish before they entered deep waters. The Indians would therefore station themselves at the outlet of the lake (i.e. where the river or stream drained it) and either spear or gaff the salmon. (A gaff is an implement about six feet long with a hook at the end.) There was little effort to use baited hooks; the trick was to spear a fish and haul it aboard in one swift, continuous motion. Some people used nets, and when the salmon were arriving at the lake in large quantities, during the spawning season, they might literally herd large numbers of them to the shores, where they could be taken.

The technique of impounding fish was generally used in the tideland areas, however, because of the action of the tides. Fish would come into the secluded and narrow parts of bays during high tide, and the people would build large pens while the water was still high. When the tide went out the fish would be trapped inside the pens. Sometimes with the smaller varieties, such as smelts or candlefish, impoundment was the only practical way to catch a large number quickly.

The most famous fishing techniques were those developed for use in freshwater streams and creeks that drained into the inlets. The salmon spent an average of three years at sea and returned to their spawning grounds and gravel beds in the freshwater streams in the mountains. Large weirs, usually community property, were built across the rivers to catch the returning salmon. Weirs varied with the width of the stream, but generally they would consist of three tripods embedded in the stream bed with brush fences between the stakes, which trapped the salmon as they swam upstream.

Once the salmon were trapped behind the weirs, the people used dip nets to take the salmon. While the weir was community property, the dip-netting platforms were privately owned by families, and one had to ask permission of the owners to use them. All the facilities for curing the fish were also privately owned. This peculiar distinction between community ownership of the means of catching the fish and family ownership of the means of preserving the fish was misunderstood for decades by lawyers involved in fishing-rights cases. They used to insist that because Indians shared the weirs they had no concept of individual property rights. But if one had no means to preserve the fish once it was caught, fishing was of little value, and the houses for curing the fish and the drying racks were individually owned.

On freshwater streams and creeks the Indians used gill nets as well. The gill nets were large nets designed to catch fish of a certain size. The openings of the mesh in the net would allow small fish to pass through it with ease, but it would snare the gills of larger fish when they tried to force their way past the net. The nets would be set in a river for hours at a time and then pulled to shore filled with fish. Generally these nets were not placed across the entire river but, rather, on alternating sides of the river every several hundred yards so that some fish could get through the nets and up the river to spawn.

In the northern part of the inland waters near the Straits of Georgia, the Lummi developed a unique kind of fishing aptly called reef netting. They would take two canoes, extend a large net between them, and anchor it on the floor of the bay or passage where the salmon would be coming. As the salmon began to swim into the camouflaged net, they would believe that the floor of the bay was shifting upward. The salmon would swim upward with the incline of the net, and at a certain point the head fisherman would shout—a signal to raise the net, thus trapping the fish.

The head fisherman was vitally important in this type of fishing, because he had to tell from the movement of the water how far into the net the majority of the fish had come. If the net was raised too soon the salmon would be frightened and swim away. If it was raised too late the salmon would be able to swim over the net, or they would have been able to detect the net in front of them and rapidly swim around it.

With such split-second timing necessary, the leader of the

fishing expedition had to have an almost mystical sense about the salmon, the water, the nets, the current of the water, and his men's ability to raise the net quickly. Reef-net fishing required an incredible sense of timing and an intimate knowledge of all the factors that affected fish life. Leadership on a reef-netting expedition was so intuitive that those men who had continued success as reef netters were considered to be possessed of a supernatural ability and religious powers over the salmon.

When the white men came to the Straits of Georgia and tried to learn reef netting they were unable to catch any salmon, and many quit in disgust when the salmon would not come into their nets. Eventually they learned how to camouflage their nets in the Lummi manner, but they never learned that special, mystical sense that the old Lummi fishermen had about the timing of the catch. The salmon never spoke to them as they had spoken to the Lummi reef netters.

Reef-netting sites were the most prized inland fishing grounds because the catch was generally sockeye salmon, considered a delicacy by all the tribes of the region. Catching sockeye meant that the Lummis could trade extensively with the other tribes for desirable goods, especially for the whale and seal oil and the meats of the coastal tribes. Reef-net ownership has proved a great aid in scholarly interpretation of the treaties. By comparing the owners of reef-netting locations with signatures on the treaties it can be determined if the Indians understood that they were giving up fishing rights. No Indian would sign any document that took away his reef-netting site, and so when we see the signatures of reef-net site owners on treaties we know that they were promised freedom in their reef netting.

Besides reef netting, the people of the sound and the straits also developed trolling, long-lining, jigging, and set-lining

A boatload of men from the Makah tribe bring a whale ashore on Neah Bay, Washington. Sealskin floats are keeping the carcass afloat, 1926 or before.

techniques for fishing. In all these methods the Indians relied upon their cleverness in designing nets and hooks for fishing that would coincide with the manner in which the salmon could most efficiently be taken. Since the salmon, in preparation for spawning, do not eat once they have entered fresh water, it was ridiculous to use hooks in the manner we do today. When the white men came into the area and saw the Indians fishing without bait it was a great surprise to them and they were even more shocked when they learned that the Indians had relatively good luck despite the lack of bait.

In the ocean and the large straits fishing was a wholly different matter. Nets were not as important, because the people were out after larger game—whales, seals, sea otters, and the like—and both skill and technique were much different. The Makahs of Cape Flattery, the whalers of the Northwest, caught few salmon but many halibut in their coastal waters. The whaling canoes would go from twelve to twenty miles off-shore to hunt the large mammals with harpoons. The canoes, although very large, were tiny beside the gigantic whales, and so the trick was to harpoon the whale while preventing him from sounding and breaking loose from the harpoon. Seal bladders, used for floats, were attached to the whale once the harpoon had been thrust into it, thus preventing the giant mammal from diving.

The Makahs used a combination of floats to tire the whale. As more and more floats were attached to it, the whale lost some of its agility, since it became increasingly difficult to swim while dragging so many floats. With a number of ca-noes surrounding the whale, the Indians guided it toward the shore, where they could finish killing it and butcher it. It was a rare occasion when the Makahs lost a whale, because they did not try to kill it immediately but, rather, used its strength to take it back to a more convenient place.

Again, with whaling, like reef netting, the leader of the ex-pedition had to be a very exceptional person in order to lead a successful hunt. Especially among the Makahs the chief whalers were people of great religious powers who knew the whales and seals and sang songs encouraging them to come and provide food for the people. Songs were highly prized and were passed down in the families from father to son as the most important heirlooms. There could be no greater insult or thievery than to steal a song from a family, and whenever someone tried to do that it created a big crisis in the tribe. One may scoff at the place of religion in the whaling activities of the Makahs, but the fact remains that they were able to beach the giant animals with tools and boats that one would have considered totally inadequate for such activity. We can only conclude that with their songs and equipment the Makahs had devised an activity that was partially spiritual and partially economic.

What surprised the white men when they came to understand the Makah whalers was the fact that they had portioned off areas of the ocean into exclusive family plots. These areas were owned as property, passed down from father to son. People had heard of dividing the lands by constructing fences and setting up boundaries but no one had even dreamed it possible to divide the ocean. But the Makahs did it. They would sight from the various landmarks on the shore and establish where lines would intersect if drawn on a map. A Makah could take his canoe almost out of sight of land, and by sighting to the different outstanding landmarks such as points of land, high mountains, or river entrances, he could tell exactly where his family's whaling area was. No one used a compass or other device to mark out the areas, because from the time each boy was old enough to ride in the canoes he was taught where the fishing areas were and who owned them.

The Chinooks who lived along the Columbia River had a unique manner of catching fish in the large river. They would construct a net some five hundred feet long and nearly fifteen feet in depth which would be placed in the river, going nearly all the way across in some places. As the salmon run began, they would gradually pull the net around to catch the fish and then ease it toward the shore. When they reached shallow water, the fishermen would go into the net with mallets and clubs, killing the fish and throwing them up on the shore. This technique involved many men and was useful only when there was a large run of salmon on the river, but in the Columbia especially the salmon runs in the old days were incredibly large, and so the device worked very well.

Perhaps the most exciting type of fishing done by the Indians of the region was flounder fishing. The flounder, a flat fish that tends to rest on the bottom of mud flats, loved those along the sound. The Indian fishermen would simply wade into the mud flats until they stepped on a flounder, and then they would stand on the fish long enough to spear it with a sharp stick. The method sounds simple, but the sight of a hundred Indians all standing in mud flats jabbing sharp sticks

Makah Indians at their fishery on Tatoosh Island, at the entrance to the Strait of Juan de Fuca, British Columbia, ca. 1900.

at their feet was enough to frighten the whites who watched them. It was difficult to believe that the Indians rarely speared their own feet with all this frenzied activity, since the spectacle was one of continuous motion amid the muddiest water in the region.

With such an intimate relationship between the people and the fish it is not surprising that the chief religious ceremony of the Indians of the area was the first-salmon ceremony, at the beginning of a salmon run. During Congressional hearings on fishing in 1964 Frank Wright, then chairman of the Puyallup tribe, described the first-salmon ceremony of his tribe:

> Since salmon was 80 to 90 per cent of their diet the Puyallup Indians held a cultural festival or religious ceremony in honor of the salmon. At this ceremony they barbecued the first salmon of the run over an open fire. It was then parceled out to all, in small morsels or portions so all could participate. Doing this, all bones were saved intact. Then, in a torchbearing, dancing, chanting, and singing procession they proceeded to the river, where they cast the skeleton of the salmon into the stream with its head pointing upstream, symbolic of a spawning salmon, so the run of salmon would return a thousandfold.

The various tribal ceremonies were variations of this basic ceremony. The Indians universally cut the salmon lengthwise and not crosswise, for fear that the salmon would get insulted and never return to the stream. Perhaps there was some wisdom in this belief, since the cut lengthwise of a large salmon is much cleaner and easier than a crosswise cut.

Barbecuing the salmon was almost universal among the tribes also. Even when the whites came into the region, the Indians refused to sell the first run of salmon to them for fear that they would boil the fish rather than barbecue or broil it. The religious nature of this ceremony is well defined, because the usual manner of preparing the salmon was by boiling in a large box using heated stones to provide the heat for cooking. But by barbecuing, the spirit of the salmon was allowed to rise with the smoke of the fire and observe the thankfulness of the people.

When the first white men came to the Puget Sound area, they saw at certain points along the shore a series of tall poles and wondered what purpose they served. They were greatly surprised when they were told that the Indians used them to hunt ducks and other waterfowl. At night the Indians would spread large nets across these poles, and at a given signal they would come out of the darkness along the shore carrying lighted torches and yelling. The birds, frightened by the noise and lights, would fly off, enmeshing themselves in the net and falling to the ground. Quickly the Indians would gather them as they lay stunned by their encounter with the net, and the harvest would be complete. It was a unique way to hunt birds and depended, of course, upon a perennial surplus of birds.

The upland tribes who lived in the foothills of the Cascades employed a similar method to hunt deer and elk. They would hunt at night using torches of pine heavily daubed with pitch. Coming on a deer or elk, the sudden light of the torch would startle the animal, causing it to "freeze" long enough for the hunters to get a clear shot at it. It seems ironic that the Indians were the first jack-lighters of deer, in view of the discredit that the practice receives today among hunters.

The Indian technology extended to woodworking also, and in this art the Indians of the Pacific Northwest may have been unsurpassed. The lands of the Puget Sound area have a great deal of western red cedar, a unique type of wood which, though easily split, has great tensile strength. The bark of the tree consists of two distinct layers, and the soft, downy inner layer was used instead of cotton or wool for pillows, weaving materials, and other domestic purposes. Indian women were very skillful in shredding the bark into thread-sized strips for weaving and sewing, and many of the clothes they wore were of woven cedar bark.

Much of the wood used in houses and for domestic utensils was of cedar, although other species of trees were often used for their specific, desirable properties. Cooking vessels were generally cedar boxes made watertight. The cedar would be

Swinomish women barbecuing salmon on a wire mesh over a trench fire, 1938.

split into an appropriate shape, steamed until it was somewhat flexible, shaped, fastened with wooden pegs, and then allowed to dry. In drying, the wood would contract and close together, making the pot or kettle entirely waterproof.

The bows used by hunters were taken from living trees, and expert bowmakers would spend hours walking in the forest looking for a tree with the proper bend in its grain to make a good bow. Usually the yew or another hardwood was chosen for the bow because of its great flexibility and strength. A glue

Women of the Swinomish tribe preparing salmon for cooking, 1938.

was made from the skin of the dog salmon, and decorations were attached to the bow, making it not only a very powerful weapon but a work of art. This glue, one of the greatest natural adhesives known, could also be used to mend split or broken weapons.

Canoes varied in length from five or six feet for a river canoe used for ferrying to fifty or more feet for a large oceangoing canoe for whaling. The whaling canoes were very sleek and designed for fast, silent travel over the waves. They were made of hollowed cedar logs with the outsides burned to eliminate the splinters. They were then sanded down, using the skin of the dogfish, or shark, if available; a series of curved grooves were made along the length of the canoe outside. These were designed to turn aside waves in a sequence and were considered an engineering triumph by everyone who saw them.

Cargo canoes were somewhat shorter and much broader than oceangoing canoes. As the canoe was being hollowed out, boiling water was placed in it and the whole frame was stretched out to a width of nearly six feet. The finished canoe could carry a great deal of material, and wooden boxes for carrying goods were made with slanting sides to enable them to fit almost exactly into the canoe bottoms. Indian canoes were probably the first container ships in the world.

When I was teaching at Western Washington State College, I encouraged students to visit the reservations and learn what they could from the old Indians. One student became very well acquainted with an old Yakima man, and the old man told him a story about the making of the large canoes.

It seems that in some of the tribes ownership of a canoe was a religious responsibility, and in order to become a canoe owner a young man would have to fast and meditate in the wilderness for many days. He was taught to sing a certain song as he walked through the woods, asking a tree to bless him with the ownership of a canoe.

If the prayers of the young man were answered, a tree would choose him to be a canoe owner and it would sing back to him. Then the young man would make a camp at the bottom of the tree and stay there to learn all the responsibilities of canoe ownership. When the tree was satisfied that the young man was worthy of having a canoe, it would teach him how to fell it and how to trim its branches. Then the tree would teach the young man a special song, and as the young man returned to his village singing the song, the tree would follow him down the mountainside to the village, where it would be made into a canoe.

The legend seems hard to believe, but the technique of making a fifty-foot canoe lends credence to it. A lot of the western red cedar of which the canoes were made grew miles from the shores where the villages were. The Indians did not have saws or axes or indeed any metal tools whatsoever. They also lacked horses or oxen to drag the large tree from the mountains to the beach and roads over which a tree fifty feet long could be brought. When one considers today that modern loggers sometimes have to use helicopters to get the same cedar logs out of the mountains, the story of how Indians got their canoes takes on added significance. I am still not sure about the actual process of getting the large trees to the beach, but it seems to me that the Indian story is as viable an explanation as any other I have heard.

chapter
THREE

THE paradise of the Indians of the Northwest might have lasted forever were it not for the strange belief held by the Europeans that a Northwest Passage existed somewhere in North America which would allow an all-season route to the Orient. In the latter decades of the eighteenth century, expeditions were first sent out in search of this mythical passage, and many efforts concentrated on the Pacific Northwest, with the idea that ships could sail eastward to the Great Lakes, the St. Lawrence River, or Hudson Bay.

Authorities disagree on which expedition should be credited with the first contact with the natives of the northern Pacific Coast. Captain James Cook's third voyage landed at Nootka Sound, in what is now British Columbia. The sailors traded some of their goods for sea-otter pelts, and when they arrived in China they discovered that the Chinese prized these furs above any others they had seen. The urge for discovery ebbed when others learned of the fantastic profits that such a trade made possible, and the Pacific Northwest became the target of many additional expeditions.

Cook's expedition had little effect on the Puget Sound tribes, of course; their first indication of the presence of white men in the area must have been when a smallpox plague swept through the Puget Sound area in 1782, decimating many of the villages. Though the sickness was unknown among the tribes of the area, they had no reason to suspect that it had come from Europeans and tended to view it as a normal but frightening course of events. Disease was to sweep through the area at least twice more before 1850, leaving the native populations reduced by nearly 80 per cent.

The next expedition to the coast landed south of Puget Sound, on the Columbia, and was headed by Captain Gray, an American, in 1788. The ship wandered along the Oregon coast, stopping at various places to trade for furs and map the various bays and inlets. John Hoskins, one of Gray's officers, remarked on the hospitality of the Chinooks of the Columbia River area:

I was received at my landing by an old chief who conducted me with Mr. Smith [another officer] to his house; seated us by a good fire; offered us to eat and drink of the best the house afforded; which was dried fish of various sorts, roasted clams and mussels. Water was our drink, handed in a wooden box with a large sea clam shell to drink out of; the chief's son attended me, opened my clams, roasted my fish, and did various other kinds of offices in which he was pleased to engage. After this entertainment we were greeted with two songs, in which was frequently repeated the words, "Wakush Tiyee a winna" or "Welcome traveling chief."

Such hospitality by the Chinooks did little good, however, for while the chief was busy entertaining the officers of the ship *Columbia*, the crew proceeded to kill one of the tribesmen, and the ship had to flee from the area. The first experience of the Indians with the Americans, whom they came to call "Bostons" because every ship seemed to be from Boston, left a distinct dislike among them for Americans.

The Spanish arrived in the Strait of Juan de Fuca area a few years later, when an expedition under Quimper landed at Clallam Bay. The following year, 1791, the Juan Francisco de Eliza expedition explored most of the inland waters, but people are still not certain whether the Spanish were looking for possible mission sites or preparing to enter the sea-otter trade in earnest. By 1792 the Oregon coast was being visited by a steady Boston trade, and some twenty-five ships cruised the coast looking for canoes of natives with furs for exchange. The Puget Sound area was still undiscovered, however, and the tribes there, although they had heard of the strange, bearded men with white skins, had not yet encountered the newcomers.

With all the ships sailing around the Columbia River and Strait of Juan de Fuca in 1792, only one expedition took the time to name any of the landmarks, but that expedition, headed by Captain George Vancouver of England, made up for the rest in this respect. He named the large island across from Cape Flattery for himself, of course, and then, beginning approximately at the present-day American-Canadian border, named numerous natural features for his friends. The volcano that guarded the north for the Lummis, Komo Kulshan, became Mt. Baker, after his third lieutenant; the bay at its shore became Bellingham Bay; and the large island south of the area was christened Whidbey, after another lieutenant. As the expedition proceeded southward, the sound got the name of the second lieutenant, Peter Puget, and the large inlet west of the present Seattle-Tacoma region became Hood Canal, after Lord Hood. Tacobud, the sacred mountain of the Nisqually, was given the name of Mt. Rainier after an English rear admiral who had been a friend of Vancouver's. The Indians, of course, were not impressed with the European terminology and continued to call the waters, islands, and mountains by their proper names.

Along with the sea-otter trade, an inland trade for beaver pelts began when the malcontents of Canada's famous Hudson's Bay Company formed their own Northwest Company and sent David Thompson overland to the Pacific in search of pelts for Europe's hatmakers. By 1789, men from the Northwest Company were arriving on the Pacific Coast and beginning to establish trading posts with the Indians of the northern interior near the present Spokane area. Thompson was regarded as one of the foremost geographers of American history, because he laboriously recorded every possible feature he could map in his various journeys in western Canada. But his treatment of the Indians should provide him with even more fame, for he was one of the most honest men ever to deal with Indians, refusing to provide them with rum when trading and always ensuring that they received a fair deal.

David Thompson's charisma was felt by both whites and Indians, and while his business partners demanded that he make a profit on his transactions he was noted for his willingness to assist both whites and Indians in their hardships. One of the tribes in the Fraser River area looked upon Thompson as something of a god, and this admiration was to cause him some trouble. On one of his journeys he purchased canoes for a trip down one of the rivers that led to the Strait of Georgia. The tribes promptly provided him with the canoes and wished him a good voyage. He and his party did not get very far, because the river was treacherous and nearly impossible to float on due to its rocks and rapids. When Thompson complained to the tribes about allowing him to travel down the river, they explained with a great deal of sincerity that while *they* were afraid to take a canoe down the river, they regarded him as so much better than themselves that they knew he could descend the river with ease!

With the coming of the Northwest Company, activity along the trading routes of the Puget Sound area greatly increased. The exchange of salmon and other foods—particularly the whale oil of the Makahs—was stimulated by the wealth flowing into the region from the commerce in sea-otter and beaver pelts. As a result, the tribes began to adapt their style of living to their new-found riches.

But there were disadvantages to the trade also. The Yukultas, a tribe that lived on the coast far to the north, received guns fairly early in the trading days, and they began making raids in the Puget Sound area for furs and slaves. The old custom of taking slaves as a result of tribal conflicts escalated into the practice of taking slaves as a means of acquiring wealth, and wars between the tribes of the Puget Sound area and the Canadian tribes increased enormously. The raids became so bad that, as late as the 1840s, the tribes of the area had stockades for protection against the Canadian tribes. The early settlers perpetuated this warfare so that the tribes of lower Puget Sound would act as their sentries in case anyone, white or Indian, became hostile!

The sea-otter trade declined in the Washington and Oregon areas because of the rapid harvesting of the little animal, and the ships quickly shifted their trade to Alaskan waters. The furs were shipped from the Pacific Northwest to Hawaii and China, where they were exchanged for goods bound for Boston and other eastern ports. As a result of this trade triangle, many Hawaiians came to live and work at trading posts on the Pacific Coast, and when the trade declined, they took jobs farther inland with the Northwest Company and the Hudson's Bay Company.

Simon Fraser, one of the partners of the Northwest Company, established a number of forts in the British Columbia region. Between 1805 and 1808, forts St. James, McLeod, Fraser, and George were all built, tilting the balance of trade to the Canadians and providing the British Columbia tribes with additional goods to use in trade and war with the Puget Sound tribes. One of the features of this expanded trade was the development of an annual fair held by the Puget Sound tribes at Bajada Point. Each year, the tribes would gather for feasting, serious trading, and a general good time, and it was probably this annual event that set the pattern for the later extravagant potlatches that were recorded by scholars in the last decades of the past century.

The inland fur trade developed into a tidal wave in the second decade of the nineteenth century. John Jacob Astor, an American fur merchant, sent a company of traders out in 1811. They built Fort Astoria at the mouth of the Columbia and began a brisk trade in furs. The same year, David Thompson descended the Columbia from its point of origin in British Columbia and was astounded to discover the Astorians happily entrenched on the river when he paddled up in his canoe.

The Astor company was just beginning to make an impact on trading patterns in the Pacific Northwest when word of the impending war between the United States and Great Britain reached the coast. In what will probably go down as one of the craftiest business moves in history, Astor sold his trade and fort to the Northwest Company a couple of days before a British warship arrived to inform everyone that war was under way. The Indians much preferred the British to the Bostons, who often took advantage of them and used whiskey to cheat them out of their furs, so Astor's move made sense in every way. It is doubtful if the American post could have withstood a prolonged British and Indian siege.

Following the War of 1812 the European nations began a withdrawal of claims to the Pacific Northwest. In 1818 the United States and Great Britain made a ten-year agreement that citizens of either country could settle in the Oregon country, as the region was called, without impairing the claims of either country. The agreement was slanted heavily in favor of the Americans, since the British saw the territory in terms of the fur trade while the Americans looked to eventual settlement of the region. In 1819 Spain withdrew all her claims to the Columbia River drainage, and in 1824–25 the Russians surrendered their claims to the area, leaving Great Britain and the United States as the sole contenders.

Almost as if the British anticipated a long-term competition with the Americans, they began to consolidate their efforts in the Pacific Northwest. In 1821 the Northwest Company and the Hudson's Bay Company merged their operations on the coast, and Dr. John McLoughlin was appointed as chief factor of their trading operations in the Columbia Basin. When the American traders returned to the area, in 1824, they discovered that the British had things very well organized under McLoughlin.

Even with all this activity, the Puget Sound tribes were not directly affected by the whites. The British concentrated their efforts in the Vancouver and Columbia River areas and encouraged settlers to settle south of the Columbia, in the Willamette Valley, thus leaving the Puget Sound region and the northern coast virtually intact under the control of the various Indian villages.

It is somewhat misleading, however, to refer to the Hudson's Bay operations as British, because people of all racial backgrounds worked for the company. Among the most numerous employees of the Hudson's Bay Company were the French Canadians of Quebec, who formed the backbone of the regular service group. Many of these people were of mixed French and Indian blood, and they lived more as Indians than as whites. A great many employees were Iroquois—primarily Mohawks from the Caughnawaga reservation, near Montreal—who, for the most part, were Catholic. It is said that the first time the Indians of Puget Sound encountered the Iroquois they were astounded to hear them singing Christian hymns to mark their rhythm in paddling their canoes.

As noted above, the old sea-otter trade had resulted in the migration of many Hawaiians to the Pacific Northwest. A great number of these people worked for the Hudson's Bay Company. While they had a great deal of difficulty in paddling the cumbersome cedar canoes, they were invaluable in the bay and inlet waters, which were more like the waters of their homelands. It was this amalgamation of races that distinguished the British operations from the American traders. The Americans tended to be mostly whites, contemptuous of the Indians of the area and interested only in a quick profit. The British sought a well-regulated trade and eventually settled at the trading posts.

To see just how cosmopolitan the Hudson's Bay crews were we have only to look at the composition of Ross's Hudson's Bay expedition to the Columbia in 1823. It had two Americans, seventeen Canadians, five half-breeds of an undetermined tribe, twelve Iroquois (probably Mohawks), two Abnaki Indians from Maine, two Nipissings from the East, one Soulteau from the Canadian plains, two Crees from the eastern slope of the Canadian Rockies, one Chinook from the

Columbia River region, two Spokanes from the headwaters of the Columbia, three Flatheads from the Montana area, two Kalispels (a tribe that lived between the Spokanes and the Flatheads), one Palouse from eastern Oregon, and one Snake slave from the eastern Oregon area. All told, the expedition had nineteen men of white blood and thirty-four Indians.

The influence of the Indians working for Hudson's Bay became most pronounced after Ignace La Mousse, sometimes called "Big Ignace," settled in 1812 among the Flatheads of the interior. An Iroquois Catholic from Caughnawaga and former employee of the Hudson's Bay Company, La Mousse was a fervent practitioner of his faith who often spoke to his Flathead friends about the Christian holy book, in which all knowledge is contained.

The Flatheads and the Nez Percés pondered this mystery for many years and finally decided to send a delegation to the East to get a copy of the book. In 1831 a group of Flatheads and Nez Percés arrived at St. Louis demanding a copy of the sacred writings of the white men. It may have been the most unfortunate voyage in Indian history, for the sight of Indians from the Far West seeking information about the Christian religion inspired a dramatic missionary movement among both Protestants and Catholics which was to destroy the solitude in which the Indians of the Pacific Coast lived.

The tribes on Puget Sound had no knowledge, of course, of the Flathead visit to St. Louis and not an inkling of the dozens of missionaries girding themselves for the trip to the Oregon country. They were busy expanding their trade with the British, who had established Fort Langley on the Fraser River in British Columbia in 1827, and Fort Nisqually near present-day Olympia, Washington, in 1833, and an extensive direct trade with the tribes of the inland waters was developing rapidly. The British encouraged the Indians to raise vegetables for trade with the various posts, and the potato was introduced by the Fort Langley traders soon after the fort was built. Thereafter the tribes cultivated vegetables as well as various shellfish beds for sale to the Hudson's Bay Company.

The chief trading commodity of the Hudson's Bay Company was the famous blanket that made it unnecessary for the Indian women to spend long hours threading cedar bark for their fibers. Almost overnight the blanket became not only a symbol of wealth but the actual measure of wealth, just as the dollar measures wealth today. Canoes, guns, knives, kettles, axes, horses, and any other items that could be traded were valued at a certain number of blankets. On the eastern side of the Cascades, where the fur trade was still fairly lively, the value was figured in beaver skins, so that a gun might be worth fifty beaver skins at the Colville trading post and thirty-five Hudson's Bay blankets at Fort Nisqually.

Not only did the blankets change the way of life of the Indians, but the manner of dress was changed drastically by the British company. Smoke-tanned hides were unknown before the coming of the whites. When the Hudson's Bay traders showed the Indians how to tan hides using that process, the costume of many of the inland tribes changed from the cedar-bark clothes they had formerly worn to the new, frontiersman leather-and-skins costume. From about the middle of the 1820s on, it was very difficult to distinguish the Indians from the traders in either dress or background, since everyone dressed alike and a great many Indians were employed by the company in one capacity or another.

For a twenty-year period, from 1820 to 1840, the Indians and the "King George" men lived in comparative peace and harmony in the Puget Sound-British Columbia region. The British always went out of their way to ensure justice to the Indians, and treated them with fairness even in legal matters.

If an Indian harmed a white man he was promptly called to account, but if a white man harmed an Indian he was called before the same officer and given the same sentence for the offense that the Indian would have gotten. Such evenhanded justice endeared the British to the Indians, and they developed a great loyalty to the British.

As the number of whites in the area increased, the resulting expansion of trade caused the Indians to become specialists in commercial matters. The Makahs, who had used to trade whale meat for salmon, and halibut for ready-made canoes from the Nootkas, now concentrated their efforts on producing oil from whales, seals, candlefish, and dogfish for use as machine oil. They made long voyages to Forts Nisqually and Langley to trade their oil, the availability of which resulted in the establishment of sawmills. These in turn required more settlers and offered additional jobs to Indians willing to live near the forts and work for a wage.

Perhaps the only indication of change during the third and fourth decades of the century was the gradual shift, on the part of the Hudson's Bay post at Fort Vancouver, on the Columbia, from collecting furs to providing implements and other necessities for incoming settlers. This shift occurred at a time when smallpox and measles were sweeping through the Chinook tribe, which controlled the banks of the Columbia River. There had been nearly one hundred thousand Indians in the Pacific coastal regions in 1800, but by the 1840s fewer than half that number were left. Their absence, of course, left miles and miles of lands unoccupied, thus encouraging the whites to expand their settlements into the various tributary valleys of the Columbia.

The Hudson's Bay Company followed this trend of moving into areas of comparatively sparse Indian occupancy and in 1838 formed the Puget Sound Agricultural Company, which began farming and ranching operations in the Puget Sound region. Dr. John McLoughlin, the factor supervising the Columbia River operations for the company, had over one thousand head of cattle, besides hundreds of heads of hogs, sheep, horses, and oxen by 1838 and developed a large business exporting dairy products to the Russians in Alaska as a sideline to the company's fur-trading functions.

The Puget Sound Indians were prosperous, happily adapting their traditional way of life to accommodate the white man's new and exciting technology, while the Hudson's Bay Company came to control practically the whole northern Pacific Coast. There were, in 1839, a mere 151 Americans living on the coast, and if one would have been asked to guess which nation would eventually own the area all bets would have been placed on Great Britain. But the missionaries were yet to be heard from.

chapter
FOUR

THE arrival of the Indian delegation in St. Louis, as we have seen, created a considerable stir among the Christian churches. Missionary ventures were at a low ebb because of the lack of success of previous efforts among the tribes of the Mississippi Valley. But now, with a definite call from the heathen for help, the churches were galvanized into action. In 1835 Jason Lee was sent by the Methodists as a missionary to the Flatheads. He spent a short time with this tribe and, when his efforts were not immediately fruitful, moved from the western slope of the Rockies to the Willamette Valley, near the Oregon coast, where he established a new mission.

The American Board of Commissioners of Foreign Missions sent Dr. Marcus Whitman to the Wallawalla country the year after Lee arrived in the Flathead country, and the famous missionary began his short-lived career as a Protestant leader in the Northwest. The competition between the Methodists and the Presbyterians, of which Whitman was the representative, was sparked by the appearance of two Jesuits, Fathers François Blanchet and Modeste Demers in 1838. A ghastly war of religious intolerance began between the Protestants and the Catholics, with occasional sniping between the two Protestant representatives during periods of relative calm. The dazed Indians were baffled that the three groups appeared to be talking about the same God but hated each other with a passion beyond the understanding of mere humans.

Intratribal religious conflict ensued wherever the missionaries had been, and the process of trading converts back and forth among the three groups, as the puzzled Indians tried to choose a winner, reduced the credibility of the church ventures to naught. The Hudson's Bay people looked on with horror as they saw the peace of their empire shattered by a devastating religious competition.

Whitman was intolerant of Indian beliefs as well as Catholic beliefs and seemed to have an inflexible personality that refused to consider the practical realities of living in a strange land. His visionary bent resulted in the "Great Migration," which he may have created singlehandedly. Feeling that the United States should eventually control the Oregon country, Whitman sent reports back to the United States urging a massive migration of people to Oregon, and in 1843 nearly a thousand settlers heeded his pleas and marched over the famous Oregon Trail to the new country.

In spite of his failure to make friends with either Indians or local whites, Whitman continued his efforts both to Christianize the neighboring tribes and to get the Oregon country settled. He might have eventually become one of the statesmen of the territory if events had not combined against him in 1847. During the summer, a severe epidemic of measles hit the camp of the influential chief of the Wallawallas, Peopeo Moxmox, and nearly half the camp died from the sickness. The rumor spread among the Indians that Whitman was poisoning them, and in November of 1847 the Cayuses attacked his mission and killed some of the people, taking the rest as prisoners held for ransom. Some of the employees of the Hudson's Bay Company interceded with the tribe and ransomed the captives, but the Americans used the incident to attack Indian villages in the Oregon country indiscriminately, infuriating both the Indians of the region and the British settlers who had lived at peace with the Indians for nearly half a century.

Because of the previous presidential election, however, the chain of events was not in the hands of local people. James K. Polk had campaigned on the platform of "fifty-four forty or fight," a slogan that meant that the British had to cede most of British Columbia to the United States or face the prospect of war in the Pacific Northwest. As a result of the hawkish campaign in the East, the boundary of the Oregon country had been established at the forty-ninth parallel the year before the attack on Whitman's mission. The Hudson's Bay Company found itself in a state of limbo, with its status as a landowner and probable citizen still undefined. Congress did not take any action to establish Oregon as an American territory until 1848, so no one in the area knew what laws pertained or who should govern the region.

The American attitude toward the Indians was clear, and in direct opposition to the former policy of the British. While the Americans claimed to recognize the Indian title to their lands, the United States did so only to make giant land purchases possible and to move the Indians to remote reservations, away from the line of settlement. The British policy had been to recognize Indian lands and waters and to set aside these lands as places in which Indians could live. They did not restrict the Indians to these small reserves, for any Indian who wished to live off the reserves had merely to settle and record his claim and it was recognized by the British authorities.

Even the American missionaries failed to understand that the best way to get along with the Indians was to treat them as equals. Many felt that the demise of the Indian was a foreordained event and that their only task was to ease the pain with which the Indians declined. There was no recognition that laws should protect the Indians or offer them a share in the coming development of the region. Elkanah Walker, one of the missionaries of early Oregon, offered this justification for his religious activities:

It seems the only way they can be saved from being destroyed from the face of the earth is by their yielding to the control of the whites, and nothing will induce them to do this but a cordial reception of the gospel, and how can this be done without the labors of the Christian missionary.

Their concern was not so much with saving the Indians' souls as with rendering them helpless to the control of the whites. It is no wonder that resentments against missionaries still exist in Indian communities today.

Immigration nearly ceased in 1849, when everyone went to California to mine gold, but the following year Congress provided an incentive for settlers in the Oregon country. The Oregon Donation Act was passed, which allowed new settlers to claim a total of 640 acres for a man and wife in homesteading the Oregon Territory. Although no formal, recognized claim on the territory had been made, the United States Government was giving away thousands of acres of land still inhabited by Indians.

Some people in Congress were aware of this injustice, and so, in 1850, the Indian Treaty Act was passed, requiring the United States to get formal agreements to land cessions by the tribes of the Northwest Coast. The act also required that the Indians be moved to remote areas of eastern Oregon, away from the Willamette Valley and other fertile areas where there would likely be white settlement.

Anson Dart was appointed to get the treaty concessions from the Oregon tribes, and in 1851 he began to make the rounds of the Chinook villages on the southern bank of the Columbia, seeking to make agreements with the tribes. The Chinooks had suffered the most from the intrusions of the whites over the previous half century. When Lewis and Clark visited the Columbia in 1805, the Chinooks were the largest tribe on the coast, totaling in excess of sixteen thousand people. The great epidemic of 1829, called "ague fever" (though it was probably measles), killed four fifths of the tribe, and the remnant in 1851 was scattered along the various streams of Oregon, living in very small groups and fearful for their future.

Even the older settlers, who had known happier times when whites and Indians lived peacefully together, felt sad upon seeing the Chinooks' struggle for survival, and perhaps it was this sentiment that changed Dart's mind from his original purpose. He signed some thirteen treaties with the Chinooks and Tillamooks that made provisions for them to keep small tracts of land in their traditional homelands instead of moving them away to eastern Oregon, which had little to recommend it.

Congress refused to ratify Dart's treaties, because they were not in conformity with the Treaty Act. Dart's letter of transmittal to the Commissioner of Indian Affairs, submitting the treaties and arguing for their ratification, is worth quoting, because it shows that he did everything possible to help the tribes keep some of their lands. Yet he recognized, as many of them did, that their situation was at best precarious.

"It is necessary to inform you," Dart began, "that the habits and customs of these fishing Indians are unlike those of any other part of our domain. It is characteristic with them to be industrious. Almost without exception, I have found them anxious to work at employment at common labor and willing too, to work at prices much below that demanded by the whites. The Indians make all the rails used in fencing, and at this time do the boating upon the rivers: In consideration, therefore, of their usefulness as labourers in the settlements, it was believed to be far better for the Country that they should not be removed from the settled portion of Oregon if it were possible to do so."

The argument that the Indians could easily adjust to the new patterns of settlement and even make a contribution to the territory did not have much effect on the policymakers in the East, as is so often the case in Indian affairs. Dart's second argument contained all the pathos of mankind's experiences when one people has replaced another with great rapidity.

"The poor Indians are fully aware of the rapidity with which, as a people, they are wasting away," Dart wrote. "[O]n this account they could not be persuaded to fix a time, beyond ten years to receive all of their money and pay for their lands, saying that they should not live beyond that period." The Chinooks and the Tillamooks, then, did not expect to survive longer than ten years and so did not want annuities after that point. If a more dismal view of the future ever existed one would wonder what it might have been! Dart reluctantly agreed with the Indians' estimate, noting, "I cannot but admit that there is great probability that only a few years will pass ere they will all lie side by side with their Fathers and Braves—the tribe or tribes extinct."

Dart illustrated the extreme conditions of two of the tribes of the lands north of the Columbia by remarking, ". . . the only males . . . are the two signers to the treaty; there are however several females—women and children yet living." These tribes lived on Shoalwater Bay and Dart described the lands as bordering those of the Chehalis and Cowlitz, tribes that were later to figure prominently in the history of Puget Sound.

The wave of settlers could not be stemmed, however, even by such reasonable men as Anson Dart. More and more Americans poured into Oregon Territory and, using the provisions of the Oregon Donation Act, began invading the Puget Sound area with impunity. Even the Hudson's Bay Company was cheated out of its lands and properties when many of its claims were disallowed because of the outcry of the new settlers. When it finally left the American territory, the British company received little more than a token payment for its holdings. Even Dr. John McLoughlin, the former factor for the company during the preceding two and a half decades, who had helped the various waves of new settlers by loaning them seeds and tools and helping them choose lands, was cheated out of his personal property. McLoughlin's declaration of his intent to become an American citizen, which should have acted to safeguard his property, was overridden by the popular demand of the new settlers for the confiscation of British property and its subsequent appropriation by Americans. McLoughlin died a pauper, in no better shape than the Chinooks and Tillamooks with whom he had spent most of his adult life.

The degree of inundation experienced by the Indians in the

Pacific Northwest can be illustrated by some of the tentative census figures for those times. In 1839, as we have seen, there were only 151 Americans in the whole area. By 1850 some five hundred Americans lived in the Puget Sound area, and two years later more than two thousand lived there. Settlement was not systematic, nor was it based on surveys of public lands. People simply arrived on the scene and started building. If there were Indians or previous settlers on the spot they were promptly run off under one pretext or another. Lawlessness and thievery dominated the area.

News traveled fast in the Pacific Northwest, and the tribes on Puget Sound and in the eastern portions of Oregon and Washington were terrified at the prospect of more whites coming into their lands. In 1852 word arrived among the tribes about the massacres of many Indian villages in California by the miners, and all braced themselves for the expected onslaught from the intruders.

The tribes east and south of Puget Sound and the Columbia were in a much better position to confront the invasion. Across the mountains were the Yakimas, Cayuses, Nez-Percés, and Wallawallas, all fairly large tribes able to mount a concerted attack if threatened. In the southern part of Oregon were the Klamaths and the Modocs, who were valiant warriors and occupied a sufficiently large area of land to be feared by other tribes and whites alike. Conflict was inevitable, and throughout the 1850s, in spite of numerous treaties signed with these tribes, there was intermittent warfare. The little villages in Puget Sound and the Willamette Valley were often attacked by whites, who feared all Indians and used the distant wars as excuses to clear Indian territories altogether.

The situation grew so intense that even Congress could no longer ignore the state of confusion in the Northwest. In March of 1853 Washington Territory was created and a new governor appointed to bring order out of the existing chaos. He was directed to sign treaties with the tribes of the new territory and to survey a new route for a transcontinental railroad across the northern part of the United States. In this tripartite role as governor, Indian agent, and railroad surveyor, Isaac Ingalls Stevens came to Washington Territory in 1853 determined to develop the country as rapidly as possible and, with this development, to foster his own career as a leading political figure in the United States.

Stevens knew nothing about the Indians of the area and had little knowledge of the history of the white settlement of the Coast. The old politeness and formality that had marked the relations between the English and the Indians were swept aside as mere foolishness, and this violation of accepted norms of civilized behavior was perhaps one of the most objectionable things Stevens represented. He never dressed up for conferences with Indians and seemed to regard all his meetings as necessary annoyances to his central task of taming the West.

When some of the experienced settlers in the Puget Sound area saw the type of governor they had, they tried to make him understand the problems facing the territory. E. A. Starling, the Indian agent for Puget Sound, offered suggestions for the Indian treaties that Stevens was preparing to negotiate. "I would recommend," he wrote, "that when treaties are made with these tribes, their future homes be all included in one reservation—each tribe having the extent of its reservation marked off—and their fishing grounds be granted them; and over the reservation, that the law regulating trade and intercourse with the Indians, and any other law relating thereto, be extended with full force." Starling saw clearly that if the culture and rights of the Indians were not protected trouble was sure to follow.

But Stevens understood neither Indians nor their culture.

In 1854 he prepared to begin treaty negotiations with the tribes of the Pacific Coast and Puget Sound, thus bringing to an end their nearly half century of relative isolation from the inroads of white settlement. The Lummis, Makahs, Nisqually, Puyallups, Quinaults, Skagits, Swinomish, Duwamish, and other fishing tribes had avoided the fur trade and the early settlements, because the whites tended to go either south of them to Oregon or north of them to British Columbia. They had nonetheless developed a substantial commerce. The Makahs, for example, had sold twenty thousand gallons of whale and fish oil for the sawmills of Olympia in 1852 and were the chief source of machine oil for the entire coast.

But it was almost as if the tribes were destined to suffer the depredations of a half century in several years. The year 1853 marked the last year of relative freedom the tribes of the Northwest were ever to know.

chapter
FIVE

As we have seen, fishing and its related activities were the heart of the Puget Sound and coastal Indians' culture. They had successfully joined the trading activities of the Hudson's Bay Company by providing foods, canoes, and oils to the trading posts. As the Americans came into the area, the tribes continued to provide foods and oils, thereby becoming essential to the initial success of the white settlers.

Had the tribes been able to continue their fishing activities they would undoubtedly have become a strong force in the development of Washington Territory. But government policy dictated two major changes in Indian life. The first change to be made was the concentration of as many villages as possible on one reservation, which would be isolated from the rest of the settlements and directed by an agent chosen because of his political influence and beholden not to the Indians but to his sponsor in Washington, D.C. The second major change was that federal policy envisioned turning all Indians into farmers. All Indians, without exception, had to learn farming whether they lived in an arid Arizona desert or in a massive cedar forest on the Quinault River, because the theory of history accepted by American society at that time said that man evolves from a hunter and gatherer to a farmer and therefore all Indians were expected to conform to the theory.

Almost all subsequent conflicts between whites and Indians in western Washington Territory and Washington State have stemmed from the failure or refusal of the United States to fulfill its commitments as promised by Isaac Stevens while signing treaties with the tribes in 1854–56. It is important, therefore, to examine carefully the promises of the treaties in order to understand the Indians' present-day appeals for rights guaranteed them in a dreadful bargaining session.

A small steamer was chartered to take the treaty-making party around the region of Puget Sound and the straits because the time was late and the expected rains and storms of December and January made travel by canoe or horseback almost impossible. The first treaty was negotiated and signed on December 26, 1854, and seemed to set the pattern by which the other treaties would be designed. The tribes of the Tacoma-Olympia region were called together at Medicine Creek, which is about halfway between the two settlements, and the treaty took its name from that site.

One of the controversial aspects of the Pacific Coast treaties was the language in which the treaty was explained to the Indians. Stevens insisted on using the old trade jargon called the "Chinook jargon," which consisted of fewer than three hundred words, including some Indian words, English, and French phrases. Chinook jargon was initially used during the early days of fur trading, when the fur traders of the Hudson's

Bay Company included people of all nationalities, and communication between groups of traders and trappers was restricted to frantic arm waving and a few phrases symbolizing goods and needs.

Owen Bush, one of Stevens' staff who attended the treaty session, was disgusted at the requirement that Chinook be used to explain the provisions of the treaty. When he was later asked to fight against the Indians a couple of years later he refused and explained his refusal as follows:

> I could talk the Indian languages, but Stevens did not seem to want anyone to interpret in their own tongue, and had that done in Chinook. Of course it was utterly impossible to explain the treaties to them in Chinook. Stevens wanted me to go into the war but I wouldn't do it. I know it was his bad management that brought on the war, and I wouldn't raise a gun against those people who had always been so kind to us when we were weak and needy.

Other old settlers testified that Stevens was less than a model representative of the United States. Ezra Meeker, an old settler in the Puget Sound area who wrote a book on his pioneer experiences, remarked years afterward, "Governor Stevens was intoxicated and unfit for transacting business while making these treaties."

The treaty of Medicine Creek set aside three small reservations for the Nisqually, Steilacooms, Puyallups, Squawskins, Squiaitl, S'Homamish, and other tribes. Stevens' original plan was to place all the Indians in a temporary reservation until they could be permanently located on farming land in a remote section of the territory. But the Indian representatives, particularly Leschi of the Nisqually, refused to budge from their traditional fishing stations, and so the three smaller reservations were created. The Squawskins (known today as Squaxins) received a small island in the Hood's Canal region, the Nisqually got a rocky and barren tract of land away from their traditional fishing sites, and the Puyallups got the south side of Commencement Bay, which is now the city of Tacoma.

The Indians refused to surrender their traditional fishing grounds, and with good reason. They had developed an extensive trade with the whites in salmon and other foods and saw their place in the territory as an important one. Stevens seemed to recognize the importance of the Indian fishing, since he allowed the Indians to keep their fishing sites as part of a planned role for the Indians in the future of the territory. In a letter to George Manypenny, then commissioner of Indian affairs, Stevens commented on the provision allowing Indians to keep their fishing sites:

It may be here observed that their mode of taking fish differs so essentially from that of the whites that it will not interfere with the latter. They catch salmon with spears in deep water and not with seines or weirs.

Stevens' knowledge of the Indian method of fishing was no more accurate than his understanding of the territory he had been sent to govern. As we have seen, there was extensive use of weirs and seines by the Indians, and they really controlled almost all the fishing then done in the territory. *The Columbian*, a newspaper published in the little settlement of Olympia, had commented the year before:

what little has been done in the business of securing the salmon, has been done solely by the Indians, through their crude method, and slender appliances, and that their lazy and worthless habits prevent a sufficient bestowal of time and attention, in furnishing any considerable quantity for export, beyond their own necessities, and what is required for present home consumption.

The failure of the Indian fisheries was not their control of the trade in fish but the fact, according to the paper, that they were not efficiently making a business out of it.

There were two interpretations of the fishing controversy even at the negotiations on the treaty, and the Indians secured a special article in the treaty to cover their rights to traditional grounds for fishing. The article has been the center of conflict in the intervening century and a quarter and is probably the single most familiar treaty provision in the nation:

> *Article Three.* The right of taking fish, at all usual and accustomed grounds and stations, is further secured to said Indians in common with all citizens of the Territory, and of erecting temporary houses for the purpose of curing, together with the privilege of hunting, gathering roots and berries, and pasturing their horses on open and unclaimed lands: Provided, however, that they shall not take shell-fish from any beds staked or cultivated by citizens. . . .

Articles of the same or nearly identical wording were placed in all the treaties negotiated by Stevens during the next two years, and almost all of them have proved controversial in their interpretation. At the time the treaties were signed, however, the whites did little fishing of note, and the intent of the white negotiators was to respond to the Indian demand for the preservation of their fishing grounds.

Following the Medicine Creek treaty the Stevens party went to Mucklteoh, or Point Elliott, where they met the largest delegation of Indians on the western slope of the Cascades. The tribes from the Canadian border south to the Seattle area were called together at Mucklteoh, and the chief Indian spokesman at that conference seems to have been Chief Seattle, who was regarded as the leader of both the Duwamish and the Suquamish peoples.

The Mucklteoh treaty set aside a number of reservations, which have continued until the present; the most famous of these has been the Lummi reservation near the present city of Bellingham. Perhaps the most important feature of this treaty was that it was a valiant effort to get all the Indians of the area together on the three reservations established under the treaty, an effort that nonetheless failed. In the region immediately east of the Puget Sound shoreline lived a number of mountain tribes that did little fishing but were known as "horse" Indians, because they had access to horses. They acted as middlemen in the extensive trade that had developed between the Puget Sound tribes and the larger tribes across the Cascades, in eastern Washington.

Though Stevens expected the "horse" Indians to come to the new reservations, they had little intention of doing so, and even as late as the First World War small groups of these Indians had not yet decided to live on the reservations but continued to live in the woods along the western slope of the Cascades. So controversial was this proposal to consolidate all the tribes on the reservations that another one, the Muckleshoot, had to be established away from the water for the tribes who were used to living on the prairies and uplands.

Mucklteoh was signed in early January, and by the end of the month the Stevens party was sailing along the northern shore of the Strait of Juan de Fuca to the curiously named Hahdskus, or Point No Point, where they were to meet the S'Klallams and Skokomish. Again the same basic provisions

61

were set out, including fishing rights and the establishment of small reservations. The treaty of Point No Point was signed on January 26, 1855, and a week later the party arrived at Neah Bay to negotiate a treaty with the Makahs.

The Makahs differed from the other tribes of the region in that they were primarily whalers and traders and thus greatly concerned about their whaling rights. The Makahs were providing almost all the oil used for logging and other activities of the white settlers and also had a virtual monopoly on the halibut trade in the region. They therefore had a great deal to lose from any cessions of fishing rights. The curious aspect of this treaty was that Stevens wanted to show a clear purchase of the lands he had designated as belonging to the Makahs, while the Indians were worried about preserving their ocean properties.

The Makahs had developed a sophisticated property law regarding their beaches. These were very precisely divided among the prominent tribal families. Each Makah house owner claimed not only a section of the beach but also any material that happened to float ashore on his property. Old men who could no longer go whaling spent their days propped up against a wooden backrest, chatting with their cronies while waiting for something to float in on their section of the beach.

Not only did Stevens fail to understand the complex nature of Makah beach ownership, but he promised the Indians more rights than the United States could reasonably guarantee. Stevens told the Makah chiefs that he did not want to stop their whaling but would see that the government sent them oil kettles and fishing apparatus to make their fishing even more efficient. "The Great Father," he noted, "knows what whalers you are, how you go far to sea to take whales.

He will send you barrels in which to put your oil, kettles to dry it out, lines and implements to fish with."

In the case of the Makahs, therefore, both Stevens and the Indians felt that the treaty would guarantee the special rights of the tribe. The article securing fishing privileges, Article Four, was essentially the same as the other treaties except that it read: "The right of taking fish and of whaling or sealing at usual and accustomed grounds and stations. . . ." The "stations" of the Makahs, however, were patches of ocean marked by their special method of sighting intersecting landmarks from their boats far out to sea. The complications of this treaty provision would become apparent many years later.

After the treaty of Neah Bay things seemed to dissolve for both the Indians and Stevens. A gathering of Indians was convened on the Quinault River, and the Quinaults and Quileutes signed their treaty on July 1, 1855, but the treaty commission wanted to get all the tribes who lived as far south as the Columbia under the Quinault treaty, and the southern tribes, the Cowlitz, the Chehalis, and the Chinooks, refused to sign the treaty. It was kept open until the following January, and a few more Indians signed it, but the large land area of southwestern Washington State was never formally ceded by the Indians to the United States.

All five of the treaties had promised educational services, annuity goods, and access to fishing, while restricting Indian trade to the Americans. Each treaty forbade the Indians to go to Vancouver Island to trade with the Canadians, because the local whites had much need of the Indian trade and because the government wished to limit the great influence the British still held with the Indians. The lands of the area west of the Cascades were declared cleared of Indian title, but in fact they would not be cleared until the treaties could be formally ratified, an event that did not occur for several years. In the meantime Stevens made a grievous mistake; perhaps it was not even a mistake, but a deliberate effort to spur a conflict. At any rate, after signing five peace treaties with the tribes of the Pacific Northwest, Stevens promptly triggered the only Indian war in Puget Sound history.

Isaac Stevens and Joel Palmer, superintendent of Indian affairs for Oregon, went to the eastern tribes of the region to get treaties of land cession from them. The situation among the Cayuses, Yakimas, Nez Percés, Wallawallas, and other tribes who lived between the Cascades and the Rockies was desperate because of the discovery of gold in the Idaho region and the subsequent rush of miners into the Indian lands. Many of the Indian leaders across the mountains refused to sign the treaties, and the spirit of war hovered over the deliberations. Yet, because of the friendship of Peopeo Moxmox and other respected leaders, Stevens was able to secure agreements with the tribes. Large reservations were set aside for the tribes and they were expected to move onto them within two years after the treaties were signed.

The settlers all over the area were waiting to invade the remaining Indian lands now that the treaties were signed, and the two Indian superintendents gave them their opportunity. They signed a joint article in the June 23, 1855, issue of the Oregon *Weekly Times* announcing the signing of the treaties in highly misleading terms:

By an express provision of the treaty the country embraced in these cessions and not included in the reservation is open to settlement, excepting that the Indians are secured in the possession of their buildings and implements till removal to the reservation.

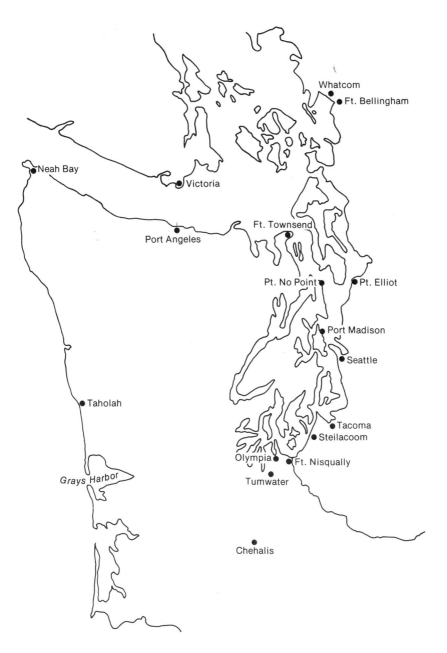

The early settlements in Washington State at the time of
the signing of the treaties purchasing the Indian lands
and guaranteeing perpetual fishing rights to the Indians,
1854.

The effect of such a statement was electrifying, and settlers began claiming lands whether there were Indians on them or not. While the proclamation had originally referred to the lands of the eastern slope of the Cascades, the whites living in the Puget Sound area saw no reason to be left out of the general land rush, and soon the little Indian settlements on the inland waters were overrun with white squatters.

Only the sparsity of whites in the Puget Sound area saved the tribes from total extinction. There were simply more Indians than whites. Yet the situation rapidly deteriorated, particularly among the Nisqually, who had been given a reservation far from their traditional fishing grounds and unfit for anything, even horse grazing. By the end of 1855, matters had come to a head, and the chief of the Nisqually decided on a course of action.

On January 26, 1856, Leschi and the Nisqually with some allies from other tribes attacked the little settlement of Seattle and were giving the settlers a very difficult time when warships in the harbor began shelling the Indian positions. As with other Indian efforts to repel the whites, friendly Indians informed on the Indian forces, thus dooming their own people to failure. The war, which curiously became known as the "Yakima" war because of the simultaneous conflict east of the mountains by the Yakimas under their great chief Kamiakin, lasted about three years and became a conflict of sporadic ambushes and skirmishes that accomplished very little for either side.

Had Stevens returned to Puget Sound promptly on hearing about the Indian troubles, things might have worked out differently. Perhaps he feared the political backlash of the settlers, for he exercised little leadership in getting the Indians and the whites together to resolve the problem of land squatting. Instead of acting as a leader for peace Stevens encouraged the fight against the Indians by organizing "volunteer" companies, i.e., groups of bandits who scourged the Indian villages. General John Wool, commander of the Army Department of the Pacific, condemned the use of the Oregon and Washington volunteers, remarking:

> their net result was to turn friendly and neutral Indians into hostiles.

A heated conflict ensued, between Stevens and Palmer on the one hand and Wool and the Army on the other, over the causes of the Indian troubles and the use of volunteers to calm the Indians. Wool argued that disbandment of the volunteers would stop them from provoking the Indians and thus restore peace. Stevens and Palmer were excited over the political benefits that the war would give their careers, remembering perhaps "Old Tippecanoe" and other Indian fighters who had once occupied the White House.

The Indian effort collapsed, of course, because with a few exceptions there were no strong ties among groups of Indians that would cause them to see the conflict as a direct threat to themselves. Leschi fled to the Yakimas following the disaster at Seattle; he was betrayed by his Indian friends, found guilty of murder in two swift trials, and eventually hanged as a renegade. Numerous appeals by white settlers who had known the Indian side of the story did not budge the new settlers, who had just had their first taste of Indian war, minor though it was, and who saw vengeance as the only way to "teach" the Indians about civilization.

About the only positive result of the conflict was the establishment of the Muckleshoot reservation near present-day

Auburn, Washington, and the re-establishment of the Nisqually reservation on lands move favorable to their fishing economy. Some historians saw the war as the last resistance of the Indians in the Northwest, but the simple fact remains that there had been no significant controversy during the previous half century, because the Indians and the whites had worked together in harmony. It was only after a great influx of whites onto the Indian lands, through Stevens' and Palmer's urging, that the pattern of life on the coastal lands was disrupted and conflict ensued between the two peoples.

chapter
SIX

THE brief war between the Indians and the settlers served to hasten settlement in some of the outlying areas of the territory. During the war, the older, long-established settlers built twenty-two blockhouses for protection, but some of these were designed to protect both Indians and whites against the intrusions of the tribes from British Columbia who took advantage of the hostilities in the Puget Sound area to raid both Indian and white settlements. The volunteers built another thirty-five blockhouses during their short time under arms, and the regular Army built four blockhouses, so that by 1856 the area was dotted with sixty-one fortifications. Around these blockhouses many settlements were later to develop.

For the most part the war did not drastically disrupt life either for the Indians or for the whites. Outside of those tribes actually engaged in hostilities, most of the outlying villages were so remote that some did not know that a war was being conducted and the others had only vaguely heard of the troubles across the sound. Thus it was that in many places in the territory there was no animosity between Indians and whites, and trade between the two continued to develop. Probably the only change was the movement of some of the smaller villages from their traditional homes on the rivers to the new reservations. A new style of life quickly developed for these people, and it would be well to visualize how they now began to live.

The largest of the new reservations were Tulalip and Muckleshoot. On both of these, people from both the tidelands and the mountain foothills settled. At first there was some difficulty in adjusting to the new life. The old villages had been very small groupings of families, while the new reservations had several thousand Indians living on them. The closeness of the different families became unbearable for many of the people, and they began to wander off to find other places to live.

This new life was particularly difficult for the mountain people. As we have seen, they had been used to a different kind of fishing in the freshwater streams and lakes, and they did not take to the idea of fishing in bays and inlets. In time they went to the agents and complained that they couldn't make a living on the new reservations, and many of them were allowed to go back to their old homes. Though the treaties had set aside only a fixed number of reservations, the agents found it necessary to establish several new ones for the different groups who refused to be concentrated on the larger tracts of land.

In the midst of the confusion caused by the setting up of new reservations without orders from Washington, a big controversy arose over whether the new Muckleshoot reservation was under the agent at Tulalip or the agent at Nisqually. The reservation had been provided for under the Medicine Creek treaty, the only treaty to have been ratified by Congress before the beginning of the war. This placed it under the jurisdiction of the agent at Nisqually. But it was actually established within the boundaries set by the more recent Point Elliott treaty, and so the agent at Tulalip felt the reservation should come under his control.

This confusion worked to the advantage of some of the tribes of the southwestern part of the territory who had not signed a treaty in 1854 or 1855. Isaac Stevens had visited Grays Harbor in 1855, following his successful negotiations with the Makahs and Quinaults of the Pacific Coast, with the idea of getting the Chinook and Chehalis tribes occupying the southwestern quarter of Washington Territory to agree to his treaty terms. But he reckoned without the strong attachment of the Chinooks to their fishing grounds. The tribes refused to sign the treaty when they discovered that it gave the President the right to move them away from their lands to a large reservation. "That little creek," one of the Chinooks declared, was the only place he ever cared for, and the treaty was not signed.

If the officials in Washington realized that much of the state had not legally been cleared of its Indian title, they made no effort to inform the agents in the field about what they were doing to correct the situation. The Indian agent at Puyallup, in writing his annual report in 1876, rather crossly noted that he had discovered a new Indian reservation that the officials in Washington had established in 1866 on Shoalwater Bay. But, he insisted,

> . . . its existence as an Indian reservation was unknown to any officer of the Indian Bureau in this Territory till I accidentally discovered it a short time before the abolishment of my office as superintendent of Indian Affairs of this Territory, and my visit to it last month was the

first visit ever made to it by any officer of the Indian Bureau.

It remains a mystery how the government in Washington could set aside an Indian reservation without informing its officials that such a reservation existed, let alone how a reservation could be in existence for ten years before being discov-

A Clallam Indian family near Port Gamble, Washington, ca. 1910.

ered. But such mistakes were commonplace in the years when the reservations were being established.

We can easily imagine the early reservation settlements in Washington Territory from the descriptions found in the annual reports of the Indian agents. For the most part the small villages of the old days were abandoned in favor of much larger villages which featured houses made in the white man's

An Indian woman and her children pose for a picture near the Clallam Indian settlement in Washington, 1910.

way, for single families, not for several families. Little log cabins dotted the lands surrounding the government agencies where the Indians could collect the annuities promised them in the treaties. An agent lived at the largest village on each reservation; he might be a farmer or a schoolteacher, but he was responsible for everything that happened there.

The little agency towns were usually designed according to the new white settlement patterns, with streets and sometimes a common grazing ground for the horses and cattle. Generally a schoolhouse was the most prominent feature of the new village because of the treaty provisions for the education of Indian children. This schoolhouse would generally have dormitories for children who lived far from the village; on the Tulalip agency, for example, the children of many of the smaller reservations such as the Lummi and Swinomish, came to stay and attend school. Each school would have a complete farm as part of its program if at all possible. This farm would include dairy cattle, fruit trees, and numerous smaller sheds and storehouses for supplies and machinery.

The first task of the new agents would be to instruct the adult Indians in farming their lands, because farming was regarded as the best means of ensuring civilization of the Indians. The agents' reports during the 1850s and 1860s are very interesting, because they reflect an unbounded enthusiasm for the achievements of the Indians in farming. But in the later years, after the agents had been working several decades to teach the Indians farming, the reports begin to reflect a great discouragement at the Indians' meager progress.

The answer to this strange puzzle is very easy to understand. The tribes, as we have seen, were traditionally fisherfolk, and they loved the life of fishing more than any other. Their farming efforts were largely undertaken to please their new agents, and thus they accomplished just about what they figured would satisfy the strange white man, who insisted that they plant vegetables and grains when common sense told them such things would never grow in so wet a climate. On most reservations the Indians spent nearly as much time fishing as they always had, except that with their farming duties they had to work a little harder, since farming took a great deal of time during the spring and early summer.

A young Indian girl resting with her baskets during the summer hop-picking outing with her tribe. Clallam settlement, Washington, 1910.

An Indian girl and her little brother dressed in traditional garb at the Clallam settlement on Juan de Fuca Strait, Washington, 1910.

Sometimes the agents recognized the great difficulty in trying to make the Indians farm, and they resented the federal policy as much as the Indians did. The agent at Tulalip, for example, in his annual report of 1879, made the following observation on the lands of the northern reservations:

The land on the Tulalip, Madison and Swinomish is of such a poor quality that it affords but little encouragement to the Indians to follow farming as a business, for with the exception of a few small swails or marshes it is high and gravelly, and thickly covered with a dense growth of fir, cedars, and spruce. It requires an immense amount of labor to clear a few acres, and even when in a fit condition for planting the yield is so small that it is truly discouraging, and would tax the continuity of a more industrious and determined people than the Indians.

But in spite of the agents' protests, government policy dictated that all the Indians be farmers, and so every effort was made to transform them even if their lands were unsuitable.

So determined was the government in Washington that the Indians be farmers that the commissioner of Indian affairs required every agent to list the accomplishments of the Indians of his reservation every year in order that some comparisons could be made about the readiness of the Indians to accept the ways of the white man. The following paragraph is taken directly from the agent's report on the Puyallup reservation in 1876 and shows just how detailed these reports were.

Over a hundred and twenty Indians have taken homesteads on this reservation, mostly of 40 acre lots, and they have among them all 715 acres under cultivation, as follows: 139 acres of oats; 47 acres of wheat; 95 acres of potatoes; 85 acres of peas, turnips, cabbage & s; 199 acres of timothy meadow; 16 acres of corn; 134 acres of cleared pasture-lands. About one-seventh of these lands have been reduced to cultivation within the last year. The Indians of that reservation also own 220 horses, 224 cattle, 60 hogs, and 26 wagons, and all have more or less farming-implements. The oats, wheat, potatoes, pease, and corn have been more or less injured and cut short by the great amount of wet weather during the last year, and the potatoe-crop has been largely destroyed by the rot. A few of the Indians have made some money by the sale of saw-logs from their claims, and others by the sale of cotton-wood bolts.

Perhaps it never occurred to the agents, facing each year with optimism, that their annual reports when viewed over a twenty- or a thirty-year period, had the same tone and recorded the same dismal results. There would be a listing of the different crops being planted each year with the concluding sentence of the report generally noting that wet weather had destroyed the crops and that the Indians had also fished, worked the lumber camps, or worked for the local white farmers to earn their living that year. What was happening was that the Indians were really living as fishermen and supplementing their income by part-time jobs in commercial activity.

The ability of the Indians to find paying occupations in the new territorial enterprises is truly remarkable. They worked as lumbermen clearing lands for the white farmers who had taken up homesteads in the forests. The agent at Puyallup in 1878 estimated that two thirds of the land cleared for farms west of the Cascades had been cleared by Indian workers, indicating that work was plentiful for the Indian men in the timber camps. This occupation seems to have been open to

Young men of the Quileute tribe resting after a hard day's work. LaPush, Washington, 1915.

Indians for many years. John O'Keane, the agent at Tulalip in 1890, reported that most of the young men on the reservation still worked in the lumber camps. Apparently some Indians must have gone into the lumber business themselves, because the Indians at Tulalip made 100,000 shingles that year, produced 130,000 feet of lumber at their saw mill, and sold 725 cords of wood to the steamboats that cruised up and down the inland waters. Such a massive undertaking was a feat in itself for people who had lived exclusively by fishing only several decades before.

Three Indian boys standing in front of the fish-drying racks at the Quileute reservation, 1915.

Farming was another occupation that attracted Indians, but it attracted them in a peculiar way. When allotments were handed out, many Indians leased their lands to whites and then worked for the whites who came to farm them. It may have seemed a peculiar way to go about farming, but it left the Indian family free to do what they wanted for most of the year. Harvest time was a particularly favorite season for those people who worked as farm hands. During the harvest a great many workers were needed for a short period of time, and many Indian families worked as migrant laborers in order to see friends and relatives from other reservations who would also work the harvest.

When the farmers began planting hops, used in the manufacture of beer and other drinks, Indians nearly monopolized the hop-picking jobs in both Washington Territory and British Columbia. Sometimes nearly the whole tribe would go hop-picking, a job that quickly became a traditional activity in the fall. Large picnics were held during the hop season, and dances, generally forbidden on the reservations by the agents, were held while the people were off working. Hop-picking seemed to replace the trading fairs that had been held earlier in the century, while the area was under British control. This pleasant ability to transform work they really enjoyed into a social event that was not really work seemed to characterize the Indian approach to life in those years.

The coastal tribes were able to maintain their fishing activities long after the tribes on the sound were forced into farming. These were the Makahs, the Hohs, and the Queets, traditionally whalers and sealers who ventured into the open seas in search of the large sea mammals. Their lands were rocky and almost impossible to farm, a fact recognized by their agents, who sought ways to help them develop their fishing as an industry.

Michael Simmons, who had been one of Stevens' assistants in the treaty negotiations, became one of the early agents at Makah; in 1860 he recommended that the government fulfill its treaty obligations and help the Makahs develop a fishing industry. "Halibut are taken in great quantities by this tribe," he noted, "and I would recommend that, in addition to the farming operations that should be commenced on their reservation, houses for salting and drying these fish should be erected, and that they should be taught to cure them after the fashion of the whites. These fish command a good price and ready sale, and I think a lucrative trade in them can be established."

Simmons left Makah, and Henry Webster, his successor, tried for three years to get the Makahs to farm. He finally came to the same conclusion as had Simmons, and he also wrote to the commissioner of Indian affairs about the tribe. "I am of the opinion that much benefit would be derived by encouraging them in their fisheries," he wrote, "and teaching them the proper method of preparing their fish for sale. By having a cooperage connected with the reservation, and supplying them with nets and salt, they could annually take greater quantities of fish, which could be sold for their benefit." The only thing wrong with the Makah fishery, apparently, was that the Indians prepared their halibut in a manner that was quite foreign to other people's tastes.

At any rate, the coastal tribes continued their fishing in the ocean waters for many years after the treaty. In 1881 the Indians of the Hoh tribe and the Queets village on the Quinault reservation sold twelve hundred dollars' worth of sealskins during the season. The Makahs continued to supply a great quantity of oil for the logging camps and machinery oil for the expanding industry of the new territory. When means were found to preserve oysters for sale in commercial markets

An Indian grandfather instructing some children on the proper way to unload a fishing boat. Clallam settlement of Juan de Fuca Strait, ca. 1910.

in Oregon, the Indians of Shoalwater Bay, the little reservation that had existed on its own most of the time, engaged in a substantial oyster trade.

Perhaps the best way to understand the period from the end of the Indian war to the turn of the century is to remember that times were hard for both Indians and whites in the territory. New machines and, later, railroads continued to change the people and the land very rapidly, and while the new lands were considered to be filled with opportunities for the industrious, the old ways of living held a certain fascination for both the Indians and the long-time settlers. The Indians worked into the new economy and the new society with relative ease wherever they were allowed to be themselves. But many problems arose in this adjustment to new ways of living, and we shall see that life was still fairly unsettled for the Indians of the Pacific Northwest.

chapter
SEVEN

WHILE we have seen the relative ease with which the tribes of the Pacific Northwest adapted to the new economy of the territory in the half century following the signing of their treaties, we have not understood some of the difficulties that stood in the way of making a total adjustment to the new life. A number of problems seemed to plague them consistently during this time, the continued hostility of the whites, in particular.

A distinction should be made between the old settlers and the new settlers and their relationships with the different Indian tribes. In general the longer a person had lived in the territory the better he got along with the Indians and the more he loved the lands and peoples of the territory. The new arrival, on the other hand, saw only the possibility of making a quick fortune, thus causing most of the ill will between the races. The Indian agent at Tulalip, writing in 1864, remarked on the hostility of the new settlers to the Indians:

> This class of our population, as a general thing, do all they can to prevent the Indians from living on their reservations. There is a strong prejudice against the Indians by all classes, without, in my opinion, a sufficient reason. These Indians are very peaceably disposed and if there is ever any serious difficulty it will grow out of the abuse heaped upon them by unprincipled white men.

The agent concluded his analysis by remarking, ". . . the military posts on the sound should be occupied at as early a day as possible in order that the Indians may receive such protection as they can afford." The situation thus had a potential for violence that would have meant using the Army to protect the Indians!

This hostility seemed to abound in every area in which the new settlers saw Indians as competitors for either land or resources, whether simple farming or timber lands, fishing rights, or the use of shellfish beds. We will see later how this hostility ripened into discriminatory laws and actions when the territory became a state, but a good rule of thumb would be that whenever the whites saw that the Indians had something they wanted, hostilities grew and pressures developed until the government allowed the whites to take what they wished from the Indians.

The agents of the Bureau of Indian Affairs often fostered this hostility between Indians and white settlers as a means of gaining favors from the whites of the neighborhood. The agent for the Puyallups, for example, began very early to agitate for the elimination of some of the reservations established by the Medicine Creek treaty so that new settlers could have the choicest lands of these tribes. "Some of these reservations contain bodies of as good agricultural land as can be found in the Territory," he wrote in his annual report for 1864, "and white settlers here and coming into the Territory justly complain that such large bodies of rich, unoccupied lands are withheld from them, and not used by the Indians."

The agent was rather blunt in his recommendations:

> There were four reservations set apart for the Indians of the Medicine Creek treaty, to wit, the Puyallup, Nisqually, Squaxin, and Muckleshoot. I respectfully recommend that the three latter be abolished or discontinued as reservations, and that the Indians belonging to said three reservations be removed to and settled on the Puyallup reservation. . . .

This attitude, that the lands belonging to the Indians and guaranteed by treaty could simply be disposed of at the whim of the government, characterized the employees of the Bureau of Indian Affairs throughout this period and continues in large part today. The result of this attitude was that the Indians were never certain when the government was going to take their lands and homes away from them, and if any single factor hampered the progress of the tribes of the Pacific Northwest in adjusting to their new life with the whites it was the realization that the agents were not protecting them.

Throughout the decades following the treaties, the Indians tried to bring the agents around to their manner of thinking about the status of their reservations. The agent at Tulalip was rather alarmed at their arguments, and he commented on the Indian view in his report of 1877. He tried to consolidate the tribes of his agency, which included the Lummi, Swinomish, Port Madison, and Tulalip into one reservation, but the Indians refused to move. "The Indians interpret the treaty differently," he wrote. "They say that the reservations were reserved by themselves as the permanent homes of themselves and children, and that the cession was of their lands other than the reservations. They therefore claim that the reservation lands belong to them absolutely, and it need not be added that the proposition to consolidate them with other tribes at another agency does not meet with their approbation."

The attitude of the Bureau of Indian Affairs was at best puzzling in view of the efforts of some of the agents to include every band of Indians in their agency jurisdictions in the available federal services. On the one hand, therefore, the policy that was advocated by some agents was to reduce the number of reservations to as few as possible, because the whites wanted the farming lands. On the other hand, agents continually sought out those tribes that had refused to go to the reservations, and when they could not get them to live on the large reservations they sought to establish new reservations for them.

Thus the agent of the Puyallup agency in 1879 made up a list of the bands and groups of Indians in his area that did not have a reservation, and he sought assistance for them. It is interesting to see this list in view of the fact that many people in the present state of Washington claim an Indian ancestry and often remember that their grandfather or grandmother lived in an area where there was no reservation. Perhaps some people claiming to have Indian blood really do have Indian ancestors!

The agent found groups of Indians outside the established reservations at the following locations:

Grays Harbor band—164 Indians
Gig Harbor Band—46 Indians on Puget Sound 35 miles
    north of Olympia

Mud Bay Band–41 Indians living 8 miles northwest of Olympia

South Bay Band–30 Indians living 6 miles northeast of Olympia

Cowlitz Band–66 Indians living near the mouth of the Cowlitz River 65 miles south of Olympia

Olympia Band–43 Indians living around Olympia

Cowlitz Klickitat Band–105 Indians living on the Upper Cowlitz river 40 miles southeast of Olympia

Lewis River Band–104 Indians living on the Lewis River 90 miles southeast of Olympia.

When we remember that the traditional Indian village of this area consisted of some sixty to eighty people and that many small villages were found scattered on every riverbank, we can see that for many years following the treaties some Indian groups continued to follow their old traditions.

Over the years, then, many new reservations were established as the agents were successful in getting new groups of Indians settled permanently in one place. Many of these reservations are still in existence today. But the agents were also occupied with the sale of Indian lands and the reduction of treaty reservations, and many of the very smallest reservations today were once fairly large tracts of land most of which were forced out of Indian hands and into the hands of whites at one time or another during those years. It is exceedingly strange that these totally opposed policies could have been pursued by the same group of people, but they were.

Adjusting to the government schools was a major problem for many of the reservation people. Almost every treaty contained provisions for education, usually in the form of promising a teacher for the children of the tribes. Few people understood what this educational service would be when the treaties were negotiated, and when they did find out what the government had in mind many Indians resisted the program. In the first place there was never any great amount of money available for schooling, and so on several of the reservations various churches operated mission schools with the approval of the government and some financial assistance from the Bureau of Indian Affairs. The mixture of church and state was regarded as proper for those frontier conditions, but it resulted quite often in the banishment of Indian religious ceremonies as part of the educational program. This practice only increased the antagonism of the older Indian people toward the white man's religion and education.

Because they faced this attitude of hostility toward their traditional ways, the Indians figured out a way to get around the government regulations and practices that forbade them to perform their religious ceremonies. They realized that the white men celebrated certain holidays and that these occasions were marked by a relaxation of the rules by the agent. On one such occasion at the Tulalip reservation the Indians asked permission of the agent to perform some of their old dances and ceremonies as a means of remembering that they had now become citizens of the United States.

The agent was, of course, delighted that the Indians under his care were so serious about becoming citizens that they wished to perform dances and sing songs in honor of their new status. So he allowed them to hold a special celebration on the Fourth of July. When the ceremony began, it was obvious to one and all concerned that the traditionalists were using the occasion to perform some of their most important religious ceremonies. At first the agent objected, but cooler heads among the whites who had come to the reservation to enjoy the celebration calmed him down and the ceremonies went on with no interference. From that time there was an informal agreement, never spoken, that on national holidays the Indians would be able to perform even the most forbidden ceremonies without punishment.

George W. Bell, the agent at the Chehalis reservation, in 1882 evaluated the tribe's adjustment to the ways of the white man; it is very instructive to read his comments on their progress, because they illustrate the attitude of the Indian agents of the past century toward the reservation Indians:

> To be convinced that these Chehalis tribe of Indians, with some exceptions, are as really and highly civilized as the peasantry of European lands, and not a few citizens of this "land of the free" you have only to visit their homes, look at their little farms and farming utensils, wagons, horses, cattle, plows, harness & c, see them laboring honestly in their own fields or in the service of white neighbors, meet with them in Christian worship, and

A group of young boys. Neah Bay, Washington, ca. 1900.

hear their songs and prayers and talks on the Lord's holy day.

In spite of their progress, Bell warned the commissioner about the Chehalis reservation: "I do not wish to represent this reservation as a perfect paradise. The serpent is here; and these people are lineal descendants of Father Adam and Mother Eve."

Other than the problem of separating religious teachings from the rest of their education the Indians were suspicious of the life of the government schools. A typical school would have about a hundred children from ages six to sixteen enrolled. For the most part these children would be members of the reservation families, although sometimes they would be from neighboring reservations. They received a basic education in reading, writing, and arithmetic for half a day and worked on the farm conducted by the school during the afternoon. While the boys were doing chores and helping to keep the place in repair, the girls were learning how to make clothes, how to keep house in the style of the white man, and other domestic skills. With this available and free work force the government schools were operated on a very low budget. After a while it became a question of whether the children were in school to learn or to keep the agency from running a budget deficit.

However, there were some good practices in the schools. In the government school at the Nisqually reservation the agent established a special position for the older Indian students so that they could participate in the administration of the school. Five older scholars were selected to assist the teacher, receiving a salary of five dollars a month, a munificent sum in those days, for taking charge of the younger students during some of the activities. This program enabled the agent and

An Indian girl showing baskets she has made. Port Gamble, Washington, 1910.

Indian boys watching one of their fellows playing a violin at the Clallam settlement near Port Gamble, Washington, in 1910.

the teacher to spend more time in actual teaching and planning of the programs, and many of the older students expressed an interest in remaining at the school after their graduation to work as regular staff.

Outside activities were encouraged by the teachers on some of the reservations, and the students often took an interest in things outside their immediate locality. At the Puyallup school a chapter of the Good Templars organization was created in 1890. This organization was one of the early popular fraternal groups of the Washington Territory and had a very large membership across the Pacific Northwest. Indian students seemed to like the group, since they quickly became delegates to the district and grand-lodge sessions of the organization and traveled to several conferences while still students.

The government schools unintentionally served as the scene of a great tragedy in 1888. The Indians of the region had no natural immunity from the strange diseases of the white men, and in the early winter of 1888 an epidemic of whooping cough swept through the government schools in the lower Puget Sound area, hitting particularly hard at Puyallup and on the Olympic Peninsula. No sooner did the whooping cough subside than the schools were wracked by a violent epidemic of measles. Indians of all ages perished in these epidemics, but particularly the children in the government schools suffered because they were concentrated in one place, where they could easily catch both diseases.

The winter saw a dreadful reduction in the number of Indians in the territory as they tried to apply their old medicines to the strange new diseases. Since some of the old treatments involved the use of steam baths and washing in cold streams, the treatments were nearly as bad as the sicknesses themselves. The agent at Puyallup described the effects of the two epidemics:

> In many cases children of the same family have had both complaints at the same time, or one closely following the other. Their systems are generally weak any way, and a great deal of mortality has been the result.

Even those students that did not die immediately of the whooping cough or measles found themselves weakened by the sicknesses so that they died of other causes. "In some instances whole families of children have been carried away," the agent sadly wrote. "I have in mind three families, each having four children, every one of whom has died."

In spite of these problems, which often discouraged the people, conditions remained fairly stable on the reservations during the latter half of the nineteenth century. The Indians everywhere made every effort to adapt their old ways to the strange and often contradictory ways of the Bureau of Indian Affairs. Agencies were continually shifted around, so that a reservation might become the center of activity for an area for a couple of years and then be abandoned when the policy was changed. Often the solemn promises of the treaty went unfulfilled and the tribal leaders were disheartened when they considered how much they had given up to secure services from the federal government.

The Indian agent for the Puyallups visited the Squaxin Island reservation some years after the Bureau of Indian Affairs discontinued its services to the Squaxins; and his report described a scene of desolation that might have softened the heart of any policymaker:

> After the removal of the agency from Squaxin, all improvements ceased and slow decay commenced there and still continues. Most of the buildings erected there by the government have either rotted down or are in ruins. Most of the cleared land is covered with bushes, except a few acres of good meadow, which has been kept fenced and is mowed yearly for hay. A few of the old-time fruit trees are still standing and produce some fruit amid the wild bushes that have grown up around them.

If the government could build hope, its departure could trigger a sense of despair as well.

With all these adjustments to their old traditions, it may have seemed to many of the Indians that times had changed permanently, but we must understand this change as they did —not as an abrupt disruption of customs but a general and gradual shifting to new ways of living. Perhaps the best indication of this gradual change can be seen in the way that the various reservations came to govern themselves. Under the old traditions the villages would be governed by the leading heads of families, who would meet in an informal session to determine village policy.

With the establishment of reservations and the necessity of several tribes' having to live on the same tract of land, the idea of chiefs became more formal as the leading men of each village gathered to represent the interests of their people in a general reservation council. When the Indian agents recognized the natural formation of informal councils of the different groups, they wisely made the council a regular feature of reservation life. Thus it was possible for the various reservations to evolve their own form of government, and this consolidation of many groups into a larger and more efficient governing body most probably would have developed in time anyway.

The Indian agent at Puyallup, writing his annual report in 1879, remarked on the establishment of the reservation council; taking advantage of the Indians' desire to govern themselves, he gave them the power to police the reservations. "I appointed a council of three chiefs," the agent reported, "with two sheriffs, to keep order, to try and punish for minor offenses, with right to special appeal to me. Such is the case with all the reservations under my charge except Puyallup, where they have a chief of police and six policemen." By the mid-1880s nearly every reservation had its own reservation council, its police force, and a system of tribal courts in which the tribal judges heard cases and levied sentences subject to an appeal to the Indian agent in cases of severe punishment or unjust sentence.

The councils were expanded or reduced in number as the population demanded. The pay for policemen was taken from the income of the tribal courts, according to the following scale: five dollars a month for privates (gradually raised to ten dollars); twelve dollars for sergeants, and fifteen dollars for captains in the larger reservations.

What is so remarkable about the Indians of the Pacific Northwest is that during the latter half of the nineteenth century they made such remarkable strides in adjusting to their new situation. They did not really abandon old ways, for they

A Puget Sound Indian family living in their tent in the summertime near Port Madison, Washington, 1905.

continued fishing whenever and wherever they could. But they also recognized the increasing importance of the new goods and materials that the white man had brought to their lands. To get these new goods they had to have an income, and, as we have seen, the people found many ways of earning an income and preserving their old ways as well.

Again, they had made an important transition from the old life as suppliers of trading posts to small reservation communities able to bring together many different skills to serve the common welfare. On the whole, life was good and except for the sporadic epidemics against which they had no immunities, which took a dreadful toll of their children, it could be said that the Indians of the Pacific Northwest had created for themselves a new life with new customs and a very capable form of self-government. Such major adjustments have been rare in human history.

chapter
EIGHT

IN the closing decades of the nineteenth century, Americans felt they were fulfilling their manifest destiny in settling the western territories. Transcontinental railroads, which had been started during the Civil War, brought thousands of settlers to the western territories, and towns grew up alongside the great railroads. Towns and cities competed vigorously for the right to become railway terminals, and the northern route, which had been a chief goal of Isaac Stevens, naturally led to the Puget Sound area. Tacoma was chosen as the terminus of the Northern Pacific Railroad in 1873, and its chief citizens spent a great deal of effort publicizing their city as the metropolis of the great Pacific Northwest.

Statehood did not naturally follow the increase of population, as one would have expected. Before the Civil War the northern and southern states engaged in vigorous competition to open new territories and admit new states to the Union.

But following the Civil War the trend was reversed, and the various territories were not easily admitted to the Union as new states. Washington remained in territorial status from 1853 to 1889, a period of thirty-six years, in which the population grew tremendously. Conflict between Democrats and Republicans helped to keep the northwestern states from being admitted. Neither party was able to decide which way the new states might vote politically, and accusations from both parties made admission of new states a hazardous venture for the leadership of Congress.

Finally a compromise was worked out, in the closing months of 1889, and Washington, Montana, North Dakota, and South Dakota were admitted as states. The impact of statehood on the Indians of the Pacific Northwest was to be immense, but few realized it at the time. It is important, therefore, that we understand how much change was really brought about by the admission of Washington to the Union.

While Washington was a territory, everyone, Indians and white men alike, were under federal laws. The governor and the judges were both appointed by the President, and, while they were often people of good reputation in the territory, there were cases in which the appointments were purely a matter of political patronage. But regardless of who was appointed, all officials had to carry out the federal laws of the United States, and among these laws were the treaties signed by Isaac Stevens with the tribes of western Washington. There was no intervening government to pass contradictory laws affecting treaty rights, and in this sense the territorial status of Washington served to protect the Indians in their hunting and fishing rights.

Washington was required to place in its state constitution a provision stating that it would never attempt to confiscate the lands or rights of the Indians without the express permission of the Congress of the United States. But this phrase in the constitution did not seem to the new officials of the state to be important, because most of the reservations had been divided into small farms by the Congress, and in the law allowing this division of Indian lands Congress had provided that a state could remove any restrictions that had been placed on the Indian lands once the period of federal trust had expired. Thus it seemed that on the one hand Indians were given a favored status in the new state and on the other hand the new state appeared to have some control over the Indians.

If the country had remained sparsely settled, perhaps the question of Indian rights, particularly fishing rights, might never have become important. But with the waves of new settlers brought into the Puget Sound area by the Northern Pacific Railroad, the problem of Indian rights began to bother the officials of the new state. Many of the settlers brought into the Puget Sound area in the 1880s were of Scandinavian descent, and a substantial proportion of these people were only one generation removed from their homes in Europe. They had arrived in the Midwest only thirty years before and were enticed westward by extravagant descriptions of the opportunities of the Pacific Northwest, fostered by the civic booster groups of Tacoma and Seattle.

The Scandinavians had a great fishing tradition, like the Indians, and the technology of canning fish had been developed to a very sophisticated science by the late 1880s. So conflict between the Indians, who had always fished but in a haphazard and non-commercial manner, and the new settlers, who fished in an efficient and commercial manner, developed. The Indians' first response to the expanding fisheries of the area was simply to fish and sell their catch to the new canneries, which were springing up everywhere. For a while this compromise seemed to work, but as more and more canneries were built the fish runs declined seriously, and soon the Indians and the whites were competing for fish on grounds that had traditionally been reserved by treaty for the Indians.

There were other developments that were just as important in the way that people began to look at Indian rights. Timber was a very important resource, and as logging camps expanded into the wilderness, hunting was reduced to a few places as yet untouched by civilization. As settlements increased, game declined tremendously. Pressure to open the unallotted reservations for lumbering began to grow, and again the question arose concerning the rights of the state government over the lands of the Indians. Did the new state have the right to open lands to settlement? Could the new state enforce its laws on the reservations if it did not interfere with the services provided to the Indians by the federal government? These were new questions, and no one seemed to know the answers.

The first inclination of the whites in the new state was to take some of these questions to the courts to get an official interpretation of the treaties by the judges. At this point a controversy developed that has not been satisfactorily settled to this day. Which court, state or federal, was capable of correctly interpreting the Indian treaties? During territorial days the courts run by the federal government generally interpreted the treaties in favor of the Indians. Now, with the creation of state courts, which were naturally inclined to support the rights of the state against the federal government, decisions seemed to indicate that state courts would favor the elimination of Indian rights in favor of the new state government.

Even the federal courts seemed to change with statehood.

Some of the territorial officials had been appointed to federal court positions when the territory became a state, while others had become elected officials of the new state. The older judges and federal attorneys, in trying to emphasize the continuity between territorial and federal law, relied heavily on territorial precedents in deciding their cases. But the situation had changed a great deal in that judicial appointments were now subject to the political approval of the new state senators and congressmen, who were dependent upon the voters for their continued stay in office.

In territorial days political decisions were often based upon the simple proposition that what was good for a continuing growth of settlement while keeping faith with the Indians was a proper decision. Now, with statehood, mixed political motives entered the picture for the first time. Even the most dedicated federal official always had to remember that he could be removed for politically unpopular decisions and that if he made decisions that were popular he could easily move from a status of appointed official to senator, congressman, or governor in a future election. Thus decisions deeply affecting Indians many times reflected the desires of the federal appointee to launch a political career sometime in the future.

We can see that many of these considerations worked to create a situation in which Indian rights became a minor consideration in a larger political arena involving a great many factors not present during territorial days. Enforcement of laws and popularity of decisions became the most important aspects of the Indian relationship with the new state. It was not long after statehood that this complex situation generated its first series of conflicts.

In February 1890, in one of the first acts of the new state, a commissioner of fisheries was created, and the following year a Department of Fisheries was established with powers to supervise fishing within the state. No mention was made in the early reports of the state fishing commissioner of any problems with Indian fishing, but that was probably because the problem made its first appearance in three cases, heard in the new federal court, that vitally affected the interpretation of Indian fishing rights, a problem still relegated to the federal government.

The treaty of Neah Bay preserved, as we have seen, the rights of the Makahs to go whaling and sealing in the ocean off the Northwest Coast. Over the years this industry had expanded quite substantially, and by the late 1880s the Makahs owned several large whaling vessels and were engaged in extensive whaling activities. In the spring of 1889 Chestoqua Peterson, a Makah, purchased a whaling vessel and named her the *James G. Swan* after a long-time, highly regarded Indian agent at Neah Bay. The *James G. Swan*, with a full crew of Makahs, went sealing in Alaskan waters under the provisions of the Neah Bay treaty. The ship was captured by a U. S. Navy ship and impounded for violating an act that prohibited the killing of fur seals within the waters ceded to the United States by Russia in 1867.

The case came before Judge Hanford, who was the federal judge of the Northern District of Washington in March of 1892. He used the case to emphasize the continuity of the new federal court with the old territorial courts and then came to an astounding conclusion about the treaty rights of the Makahs. After reviewing the treaty of Neah Bay, Judge Hanford remarked: "It is obvious, however, from the language above quoted, that the treaty secures to the Indians only an equality of rights and privileges in the matter of fishing, whaling, and sealing. The guaranty is of rights in common with all citizens of the United States, and certainly such treaty stipulations give no support to a claim for peculiar or superior rights or privileges denied to citizens of the country in general."

This interpretation was incredible in its implications. The judge appeared to be saying that the treaty promised only that when fishing laws were finally created, Indians would not be automatically banned from fishing, that they had the rights of any citizen. The decision flew in the face of the territorial laws and reversed the manner in which the Stevens treaties had traditionally been interpreted for nearly forty years. At this point the story becomes somewhat fantastic. Four years later a U.S. attorney brought a suit against a man named Winans and several others who were preventing the Yakima Indians from fishing in the Columbia River in eastern Washington. The case was heard in the federal court for the Southern District, and the judge turned out to be Judge Hanford, who promptly ruled against the Yakimas, using the same arguments he had used against the Makahs four years earlier.

William Brinker, then United States attorney for Washington, refused to believe that the treaties had done nothing more than guarantee equal treatment of Indians and whites, and so, the next year, on receiving complaints from the Lummis, in northern Washington, he filed suit on their behalf against the Alaska Packers' Association, which had practically confiscated the traditional fishing grounds of the Lummis at Point Roberts. The case was filed in the Northern District, where, it was felt, the decision would be more favorable. But who should appear as judge? None other than Judge Hanford, who ruled against the Indians for the third time in five years, using almost identical language.

Testimony given by witnesses in the *Alaska Packers' Association* case was strangely contradictory. In general the white witnesses testified that they had never seen any Indians fishing at Point Roberts, at least any Lummis, and the Indian witnesses swore that the place was a traditional fishing site of the tribe. To give some idea of the extent of the fishing controversy, one of the whites, a Mr. Adams, testified that in 1893 he had purchased 62,799 salmon from the Indians at Point Roberts and had paid $5,180.74 for them. This averages about eight cents a fish, and the fish, sockeye salmon, usually ran about fifteen pounds each. If the Alaska Packers had not outrightly taken the Indians' fishing rights, they had certainly underpaid the Indians to such an extent that these rights became virtually worthless.

Hanford's decision affected not only the Makahs, Lummis, and Yakimas, but all the fishing tribes of the Northwest, who now witnessed the virtual abrogation of their treaties by the newly established state government.

We are not privileged to know what happened behind the scenes in the federal government, but suddenly the decision was made to appeal the Yakima case to the Supreme Court and allow the Makah and Lummi cases to stand as final decisions. The *Winans* case was appealed by the U.S. attorney and was finally decided by the United States Supreme Court in 1905, nearly a decade after it was first decided by Judge Hanford.

The Supreme Court, of course, had no political considerations involving Washington state whatsoever, and it gave a very strong decision favoring the Indians, which has become the definitive precedent in the history of Indian fishing-rights law. "The treaty was not," the Supreme Court said, "a grant of rights to the Indians, but a grant of rights from them—a reservation of those not granted." The court thus agreed, as we have seen, with the arguments used by the Indians at Tulalip against consolidation of their lands. The subsequent history of the Indian fishing-rights struggle has seen this strange alignment many times. The Supreme Court and the reservation people seem to hold the same theory of how a treaty is to be interpreted, and the white population and the state and lower federal courts often hold the oppositive and incorrect view.

At any rate, the fact that the Supreme Court had interpreted the Stevens treaty phrases in line with the record of negotiations of the treaty and in line with former decisions made when Washington was a territory left little impression on state officials or the general non-Indian populace. From 1905 on, Indians would be in court almost continuously trying to defend their fishing rights against the intrusions of the white fishermen. For all practical purposes, the Lummis and Makahs had lost their fishing rights until another day, when they could get a review of their disastrous decisions. Their struggle was made much more difficult in that, though Judge Hanford's interpretations were wrong, their cases, for some strange reason, were not appealed.

While keeping in mind the endless conflict over fishing rights that began in the 1890s and continue until the present time, we must now turn our attention to the fate of individual tribes who had to fight another continuing struggle. The region was still being settled, and the drive for additional lands was ever present. In the succeeding chapters we shall see how a number of tribes lost a great portion of their lands when they were unable to get the federal government to protect them, thus falling victim to the drive for total settlement of the area. We shall examine the struggles of the Lummis, the Nisquallies, and the Puyallups against the land speculators and the Bureau of Indian Affairs, who sought to take their lands.

Before we look at the fate of individual tribes, however, we must recognize that for the Indians the admission of Washington to the union as a state meant the end of an important era of peace and friendship with both their white neighbors and with the federal government. Thereafter the treatment of the various tribes would bring about a great sense of resentment over the generations and create in the Indians of the Pacific Northwest a fear and mistrust of white society and political institutions. Many of the problems of today come from the injustices suffered by these people in the first decades of statehood, and it is difficult, even today, for Indians to forget what happened in those early years.

chapter NINE

THE Puyallups were one of the major villages that signed the treaty of Medicine Creek. Under this treaty they were given a reservation that consisted of 18,050 acres going from the eastern shore of Commencement Bay eastward toward Mount Rainier. Since the reservation covered almost the same area as did their aboriginal villages, the Puyallups experienced few disruptions in their lives as a result of the treaty. In the years following the treaty, they provided fresh salmon to the new settlements around Puget Sound and began farming and raising cattle.

As is evident from the Indian agent's reports, the farming ventures of the Puyallups were fairly successful over the years and they had one of the first and largest of the reservation police forces in the western area. The Presbyterian church established one of the first missions to the Indians among the Puyallups, and over the years a very strong church congregation grew up on the reservation. Even today, the majority of the people are nominally Presbyterian.

Since the policy of the government was to teach the Indians farming, the Puyallups tended to settle on the eastern portion of their reservation, where the lands were rolling and capable of being cultivated. They still maintained a large fishery on the shores of the bay but allowed the lands on the bay to remain uncultivated because they were hilly and because the natural materials for building smokehouses and preserving fish grew in abundance on the slopes of the shores of the bay. When the reservation was divided into small tracts of land under the allotment program initiated under presidential order in January of 1886, the people were given forty-acre tracts of farm land on the eastern border of the reservation and eighty acres of wilds or wooded lands on the western portion of the reservation as their share in the tribal lands. An agency tract of 585 acres was reserved for school purposes.

The Puyallups were generally regarded as one of the most progressive and stable Indian communities in the Pacific Coast region. They did not wait for the government to provide things for them but often took the initiative in getting things done. For years they were connected with the town of Puyallup by a ferry that took their wagons across the Puyallup River, and they petitioned the government to build a bridge for several years. When the bridge was not built, they decided to build it for the government although under the treaty it normally was the responsibility of the United States to provide such things as roads and bridges.

The tribal leaders met with a delegation of local white settlers and officials of the county and worked out a suitable compromise. The tribe agreed to provide one thousand dollars, the local farmers who also needed the bridge gave five hundred dollars, and the county gave fifteen hundred dollars.

In 1887 the bridge was built, enabling both the Indians and the local white farmers to get their farm produce to market in Puyallup. The Indian community participated in other local activities and made many contributions to the social life of the county. They had a very good brass band with military uniforms which took part in county and sometimes state celebrations and was generally regarded as one of the best bands in the state.

By all reasonable measures of adjustment the Puyallups had become useful and friendly citizens of their local community. But fate played a very ironic part in the lives of the Puyallups. The towns of Puyallup and Tacoma had originally been chosen as sites for small trading communities due to their proximity to the Puyallups, who provided a significant amount of trade for the newly arrived white settlers. Over the years both Tacoma and Puyallup had grown immensely, and by the 1890s real estate agents were enviously eying the plush Puyallup lands.

In 1886, when the government divided the Puyallup lands into small allotments, the Indians were restricted from selling their lands until such time as Congress removed the restrictions on sale. But in the same act that gave the President authority to divide the Indian lands was a clause giving the state legislatures the right to remove the restrictions on the sales of Indian lands with the permission of the Congress. In other words, if the officials in Washington could be convinced that the Indians were capable of selling their lands and making good use of the proceeds the states could simply merge the Indians into the general population.

A combination of real estate agents in Tacoma realized the bonanza that would result if they could get the Indian lands on the local real estate market, and they began to plan how they could accomplish this end. Recruiting two Puyallups as their representatives, the real estate combine began to secure leases on the various Puyallup farms. The plan was very tricky and very illegal and depended as much upon the willingness of the two Puyallups to lie to their own people as on the dishonesty of the whites to misrepresent the situation to federal and state officials. In this story there were no heroes, only unfortunate victims of man's greed.

Under the allotment act that divided the Indian lands there were provisions allowing Indians to lease their individual holdings for a period of no longer than two years. The real estate contracts provided that the Indians would lease certain of their lands for a period of two years with the right of the person holding the lease to renew it for as many succeeding two-year periods as he wanted. But the leases also had the provision that if any of the lands were taken out of restricted, federal status the leases would become deeds of sale and the lands would become the property of the leaseholder. In this way the real estate combine hoped to get around both the federal laws and the treaty of Medicine Creek, which made such sales illegal.

As soon as the leases had been made, the real estate people began pressuring the state legislature to pass a law removing the restrictions against sale from the Puyallup lands. The idea was that if the state acted swiftly and decisively the officials in Washington would feel that they had no choice but to agree to what had been done. And the choicest of the Puyallup lands would fall into the hands of the speculators. The people in Tacoma were especially anxious to get their hands on the Indian lands. The Puyallups owned almost half of the shoreline of Commencement Bay, and the natural growth of the city of Tacoma would be to expand completely around the bay because of the city's large shipping interests.

The Northern Pacific wanted the Puyallup lands to establish a better route into Tacoma, and they especially wanted the school lands of the agency in order to build additional switching and terminal facilities. As the pressure grew for the sale of the Puyallup lands, lawyers for the railroad dug up a questionable agreement made between General Milroy, who had been agent for the Puyallups in 1876, and the Northern Pacific representative, by a strange coincidence a General Sprague.

What had apparently happened during the first years of the territory is that Milroy and Sprague had signed an agreement whereby the Northern Pacific could use the Indian lands for a railway to the Puyallup coal fields some miles east of the reservation. The two men had signed the agreement in violation of federal law but had gotten a council of the Puyallups to agree to the terms. The only promises made in the agreement by the railroad were that it would pay any damages it caused and:

> That during the construction of said branch line prefer-
> ence will be given in the employment of Indian laborers,
> over white and Chinese laborers, when the Indian labor-
> ers will perform the work required to be done as well and
> as cheaply as it would be done by white or Chinese la-
> borers.

Needless to say, few Indians were hired by the railroad, because the company was always able to get the Chinese laborers to work better and more cheaply than either the whites or the Indians.

But the railroad had never had the nerve to try to get the agreement ratified by the Congress, because it apparently did not want the deed to receive any more publicity than it already had. In 1885 Agent Eells of the Puyallup reservation wrote to the commissioner of Indian affairs about the alleged "agreement" and implied that the agreement had not been fulfilled. Commissioner Atkins, in his reply, seemed to indicate that the whole matter should be left alone. But this shady history of the alleged agreement with the Puyallups made the railroad even more eager than the real estate combine to get the matter settled as quickly as possible.

The result of all this agitation was that a special commission was appointed to go to the Puyallup reservation to investigate the conditions of the Indians and make a report recommending how the matter should be resolved. A commission of three men was appointed; they arrived in Washington State in January 1891 and went directly to the reservation, where they contacted Indian Agent Eells and began their inquiry. The Indians, and even people in the Bureau of Indian Affairs, hoped that the commission would get to the bottom of all the excitement among the Puyallups.

But the commission had other ideas. It is not possible to trace whether or not the real estate agents or the railroad or both influenced the commission, but their actions on the reservation made it highly likely that they had already decided to slant everything in favor of immediate sale of the reservation lands to the real estate combine. They discovered that there were already 146 contracts signed on some 9,200 acres of Indian lands, but they did not regard the contracts as illegal. The total amount of money paid to the Indians at that point was some $30,000, and the commission itself estimated that the eventual payments under the contract would be some $700,000. They reported to the commissioner of Indian affairs that they regarded the contracts as valid.

The commissioner was very angry at their report, and he wrote an angry letter to the Secretary of the Interior denouncing the commission and its report. "On reading the report of the Commission," Commissioner of Indian Affairs Thomas J.

Morgan wrote, "my first and deepest impression was that of profound disappointment at the results. I feel constrained to say that the work done by the Commission is not at all satisfactory."

When one examines the report handed in by the commission members, the anger of the commissioner seems entirely justified. They deliberately changed their instructions to investigate the conditions on the reservation by adopting their own interpretation of the law under which they were appointed. The commission members gathered the frightened Indians at one meeting and asked if any of them were dissatisfied with their land contracts. "In reply to the sixth question, whether any allottees who have made such contracts are dissatisfied with the contracts and wish them set aside," the report noted, "we have not been able to get definite answers from all or any considerable number of them. A few say they are dissatisfied. Quite a number say they are satisfied; but most of them appear to be afraid to say."

Because the Indians were afraid to complain against the conditions on the reservation, the commission members used their fear as the excuse they needed to fail to investigate the conditions under which the contracts had been made, noting, ". . . if the Indians were afraid, or even disinclined, to say among themselves whether they were dissatisfied with their contracts, they would hardly have been communicative to us in regard to the circumstances under which they made them." One would have thought that the duty of the commissioners would have been to question the real estate agents about the contracts if the Indians refused to talk.

But the commission moved with a perfect excuse about why they had refused to talk with the real estate agents. "To get at the real truth in that regard," the commission report stated, "both parties to the contracts should have been examined. The examination of either alone would have furnished one-sided statements, which would probably be misleading if not untrue. As we did not interrogate the Indians, we saw no reason for interrogating the white men with whom they had made contracts." The commissioners therefore filed a report on the Puyallup lands without talking seriously to either the Indians, who were apparently selling the lands, or the real estate agents, who were apparently purchasing the lands. When the local newspapers started to inquire exactly who the commission was talking with, the commissioners refused to discuss any of their business, thus keeping the whole investigation from the eyes and ears of the general public also.

The commission based its recommendation that the lands be taken out of restriction on very suspicious reasoning. They had been sent out to determine if the Puyallups were being cheated or not, and their reply was a classic example of double talk. "We can not see any good reason why, for a community of only 600 Indians," the report announced, "there should be held a great body of land that stays the growth of a city of 40,000 people, if a way can be devised, without injustice to the Indians, to open it to the acquisition and occupancy of all who may be able and willing to pay a fair price for it, particularly when the Indians are very desirous to sell."

Commissioner Morgan had a ready answer to the commission's contention that the Indians were ready to sell. In his letter to the Secretary of the Interior, Morgan commented: ". . . that the Indians are happy in this trade is no more valid as an argument for its consummation than is the happiness of the child who is led to barter a diamond ring, of whose value it is ignorant, for a stick of candy that appeals to its appetite." Commissioner Morgan had understated the Indians' knowledge of the true value of their lands by quite a bit. The Bureau of Indian Affairs evaluated the reservation lands at $273.50 per acre on the average, and the commission was willing to allow the lands to go for the $700,000 price, or $75 an acre.

But there was an additional fraud involved in the proposed land sales. The commission classified the western reservation lands, those on the shoreline of Commencement Bay, as "wild and unoccupied" lands and therefore of little value. Commissioner Morgan pointed out that in the very instructions given by the Secretary of the Interior to the members of the commission prior to their departure for the Puyallup reservation it was stated, ". . . some of the lands are said to be worth as high as $6,000 an acre, while the water front alone has been estimated to be worth millions of dollars." Morgan expressed profound skepticism that the commission could overlook its own instructions and appraise the lands so low.

It seemed as if the Puyallups were doomed from the start, however, because when all the confusion was finished it turned out that everyone had been against them from the very beginning. The two Indians who were working with the real estate agents collected their fees and attended the final meeting of the commission members with the tribal community. Even Agent Eells was openly siding with the commission in their effort to cover up the real truth. As the final meeting ended, Agent Eells, in what is a remarkably preserved aside taken down by the secretary to the commission, whispered to the commissioners, "It would be a good plan to let them shake hands with you as they pass out."

In spite of the best efforts of Commissioner Thomas Morgan, who tried to stop the exploitation of the Puyallups two years later, the United States Congress, using the inaccurate report as its justification, passed a law that required the sale of almost all of the Puyallup reservation. The Northern Pacific Railroad Company got its mysterious and illegal agree-

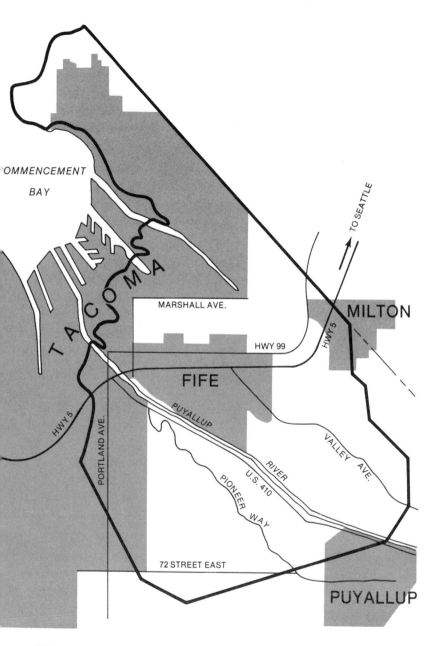

The original Puyallup reservation superimposed over a map of modern Tacoma, Washington.

ment ratified, and only the lands not used for the cemetery, some of the school grounds, and the homes of the Indians were not sold to the real estate people in Tacoma. The law further provided that those Indian lands held by the people on the eastern side of the reservation could be sold after ten years.

The one thing the law did not do was to extinguish the boundaries of the Puyallup reservation, and we shall see later that this omission made a very interesting legal point a couple of years ago. But the loss of so much land caused the Bureau of Indian Affairs to neglect the Puyallups after that, because they argued that their real task was to preserve the lands of the Indians and the Puyallups had no lands left. Following the final sales of the Puyallup lands, the state fish and game wardens began arresting the Indian fishermen in spite of the provisions of the Medicine Creek treaty, arguing that the Puyallups had only the right to fish on their reservation and that they had no reservation left. Thus the tribe that once ruled the waters of Commencement Bay and the Puyallup River was reduced to a small group of Indians huddled in poor housing on the banks of the river, on scattered tracts of land not worth selling.

Today only about thirty-five acres of land remains in the hands of the Puyallups, and it is a cemetery; some of the alottees still have small tracts covering about three hundred acres, but these lands belong to families and not to the Puyallup tribe itself. Tacoma, of course, has greatly expanded, and the real estate agents made a great deal of money from the helpless Indians. The tragedy of the Puyallups is not so much that they lost their lands but that members of their own tribe helped others to get their lands and that the protection promised them by the United States at the signing of the Medicine Creek treaty turned out to be nothing at all.

chapter
TEN

THE tribes of the Medicine Creek treaty seemed doomed. Of the three major groups signing the treaty—the Puyallups, the Nisquallies, and the Squaxins—only the Squaxins were to keep their reservation intact. The Nisquallies and the Puyallups had their ancestral lands torn from them by the government. Like the Puyallups, the Nisquallies had long been friends to the white settlers. Their traditional lands were situated on what became known as the Nisqually prairie.

The prairie was a lush and rolling meadow and proved so fertile that the Hudson's Bay Company chose the site for its agricultural ventures when the fur trade began to ebb. The Puget Sound Agricultural Company was established in 1838 by Dr. John McLoughlin as part of the diversification of the activities of the Hudson's Bay Company. Fort Nisqually, built in 1833 for the fur trade, proved to be the community center around which the British settlers gathered. After the area was ceded to the United States following the agreement on the Oregon Territory, the claims of the British to the lands of the Nisqually prairie continued and were finally settled in the 1870s, long after the old settlers had passed on.

By the time of the American treaties the Nisquallies were well acquainted with the agricultural exploits of the settlers. They had themselves begun to raise crops, and many of the Nisquallies had large herds of horses and cattle. Fort Nisqually became Fort Steilacoom in 1849, when the Americans began to rush into the lower Puget Sound region; it was generally regarded as the most important military post in Washington Territory west of the Cascades, because of its long history as a trading post and gathering place.

While the Nisquallies had a long history of friendship with the British, they were not very fond of the Americans. Holding the major part of the rich prairie lands and owning fishing rights along the Nisqually River, which emptied into the southernmost part of Puget Sound, the Nisquallies felt the intrusions of the American settlers much more than did the other tribes of the region. Everyone who came to Washington Territory seemed to pass through the lands of the Nisquallies.

In 1854, when Isaac Stevens called the tribes together to sign the Medicine Creek treaty, the influence of the Nisquallies was such that the Indians gathered at little Medicine Creek, in the heart of the Nisqually lands. Stevens asked each chief to make a map of his country so that he could put the maps together and determine where he would place the reservations. Leschi, then chief of the Nisquallies, immediately suspected Stevens' motives and refused to finish his map. Had it not been for the tact of George Gibbs, Stevens' assistant, who was very friendly to the Indians, a war might have broken out then and there between the Nisquallies and the Americans.

When Stevens designated the land that was to be the Nisqually reservation, emotions grew even more tense. He had chosen a rough, rocky plain far away from the Indians' traditional fishing sites and even some distance from their prairies. The new reservation was unfit for anything, and the Nisquallies immediately protested. Stevens departed for the other treaty meetings without offering any compromise to the Nisquallies, and the rumor quickly spread that Stevens was determined to confine the Indians in a reservation of eternal gloom, aptly called by the Nisquallies "Polakly Illahe." Conflict was building even while Stevens was sending optimistic reports back to Washington, D.C., about his success in negotiating with the Indians west of the Cascades.

As the Indians became more terrified of Stevens' real plans, word came from the eastern part of the territory that the Yakimas had begun to fight the Americans. On January 26, 1855, Leschi gathered a force of Nisquallies and Klickitats and, as we have seen, attacked the little settlement of Seattle, ultimately with little success. Due to the treachery of fellow Indians and to the superiority of American naval strength, Leschi's attempt to repel the settlers failed. Nevertheless, Indian pressure was brought to bear at the conference of August 1856 at Fox Island, where Stevens finally relented and set aside a good reservation for the Nisquallies.

But things had gone too far for Leschi. He was captured in the fall of 1856, shortly after the Fox Island conference, and was placed on trial by the settlers for murder. His old friends from the Hudson's Bay Company worked hard to save him, because they felt that the Nisquallies had had ample provocation for war in the manner in which Stevens had disregarded their complaints. Even the military officers who had fought against Leschi appealed for his life, contending that he had been captured during a period of war and was therefore a prisoner of war and should not be tried by a civil court for acts committed during military hostilities.

Leschi's old rival Chief Seattle entered an eloquent plea for Leschi, mustering the most simple logic one could imagine:

> Leschi rebelled against bad treaty. White man gives Leschi's people new treaty. White man must know, in his heart, that first treaty was unfair. Or why give new treaty?

The old Duwamish chief felt that if Stevens had admitted his error at Fox Island and drawn up a new and better reservation for the Nisquallies, then Leschi's reason for starting the war against the whites was fully justified. But the settlers saw in Leschi a spirit of independence and rebellion that they did not wish to encourage among the Indians, who still outnumbered them.

On February 19, 1858, after several trials and many appeals by both whites and Indians had been turned down, the settlers hanged Leschi for his part in the war of 1855–56. The greatest Indian patriot of the Puget Sound region went to his death secure in the knowledge that in his rebellion and fight against overwhelming odds he had secured a suitable reservation for his people. It was, perhaps, little enough satisfaction, since in later years many of those who had been so determined to convict Leschi for murder admitted that he probably had not even committed any killings.

The original Nisqually reservation had contained a mere 1,280 acres about two miles west of the mouth of the Nisqually River in an area of steep cliffs covered with a dense underbrush. During the Fox Island negotiations this reservation was changed and the Nisquallies received a new reservation, on the grassy meadow along the Nisqually River east of the old reservation, containing some 4,717 acres. The new area was part of the lands the Nisquallies had traditionally used for their horse herds, and so it was much more acceptable to the people.

Life on the Nisqually reservation was about the same as life in other small communities during the latter half of the nineteenth century. The Indians had long since learned about farming and ranching, and they engaged in those activities as a supplement to their fishing. Their horse herds grew and their farms blossomed, and of all the Indian villages west of the Cascades the Nisquallies were perhaps the most successful in adjusting to the new ways of the white man.

As we have seen earlier, the Nisqually school was so advanced that students were hired as assistants to the teachers, receiving as a salary a sum equal to that received by the Indian police, five dollars a month. The problems that occurred with some frequency at other reservations never seemed to plague the peaceful Nisquallies. In 1884 the Bureau of Indian Affairs began to survey the Nisqually reservation so that it could be divided into allotments for trial members in accordance with then-existing government policy. The idea behind this division of tribal lands, as we have seen, was to use the magical powers of ownership of private property to further civilize the Indians, and the Nisquallies were among the first to come under the new policy.

An indication of how cohesive the Nisquallies were as a community may be their reaction to the allotment of their lands. After the government agent had marked off the individual allotments and informed each tribe member where his lands were and what the Bureau of Indian Affairs expected of him, the Nisquallies held a community meeting. They had never been faced with individual ownership of lands before, and the idea was very foreign to their customs and to their religion. Land, like water and air, could not be divided, according to their understanding, because the Great Spirit had created it, not man, and He had not wanted it divided among men as if it were a thing. It was a living being, the mother of mankind, and had to be treated as such.

The problem the community faced, therefore, was to avoid antagonizing the Indian agent and at the same time avoid violating their deepest convictions. So they fenced off the entire reservation with rail fences and used the whole 4,717 acres as a common pasture for the community. Inside the rail fence individual families fenced off their garden plots and homesteads so that the cattle and horses would not destroy their gardens. The agent, of course, was baffled at the Nisquallies' solution to the problem and wisely decided to let well enough alone. For over forty years the Nisquallies maintained a common pasture; their fence marked off their little community and way of life from the rest of the territory with its hustle and bustle.

Unlike their neighbors the Puyallups, the Nisquallies were not close to the expanding centers of population such as Tacoma and Seattle, and there was no reason to suppose that they would ever fall victim to the land speculators who were quite prominently at work in the Puget Sound area. But such was not the case. By mid-1916 war fever was in the air and everyone expected the United States to become involved in the European war. Speculators were well aware that a dollar was to be made in land during the war.

In December of 1916 Jesse O. Thomas, Jr., and Stephen Appleby of Tacoma went to the nation's capital and had a quiet meeting with the Secretary of War. They promised to secure seventy thousand acres of land for the Army in Pierce County, Washington, in return for the Secretary's promise to build a fort and maintain a division of men in the county.

Land prices would boom, of course, and the profits to Ta-coma businessmen in supplying the fort would be enormous. All they had to do was build the patriotic fever to a hysterical pitch and then present their plan.

As war approached, patriotism escalated in Tacoma and soon it was an accepted conclusion that the only proper way to win the war in Europe would be to have a division of men stationed near Tacoma. The county authorities began a pro-gram of condemnation of lands to be given to the Army for the fort, and those landowners who understood what was hap-pening seemed to receive generous appraisals of their lands while those who showed some hesitancy at the program seemed to receive somewhat lower valuations. The program went very smoothly until it reached the boundaries of the Nisqually reservation.

Indian land was, of course, land held by the United States for the Indians and it could not be taken over by county au-thorities without the permission of Congress. So a careful pro-gram had to be devised to seize the lands under the guise of patriotism with the thought that in the general frenzy of war fever certain legal niceties could be overlooked. The first move against the Nisquallies was a tour of the reservation by General Burr of the Army and the Nisquallies' agent from the Bureau of Indian Affairs. The general strutted about the riverbank solemnly explaining the situation to the Indian agent and remarking that he was concerned primarily for the safety of the Indians should the fort be established.

A panicked agent wrote to the commissioner of Indian affairs in December 1917 about his tour with the general:

An investigation of the grounds in company with Gen-eral Burr showed that the safety of the Indians during the hours of target practice would require the removal of the

Indians from both the upland and the river bottom, to avoid ricocheting shells; that is, the entire reservation would have to be abandoned during those hours.

The agent rather innocently informed the general that it would be a good idea to try to lease the lands from the Nisquallies for the duration of the war, because the provisions of the Medicine Creek treaty and the price in lives that the Nisquallies had already paid for their lands was more than the Army or Pierce County could afford. The agent might have simply stated that under no conditions would the Indians have parted with their lands but, since the war fever was intense in Tacoma, he dared not say anything that might be interpreted as hostile to the war effort.

The general reported on the tour to his superiors, and a series of letters began to pass back and forth between the Departments of War and of the Interior concerning the necessity of giving up the Nisqually lands for Fort Lewis. The Interior Department was in favor of leasing the lands to the War Department, while the Army and the businessmen in Tacoma were intent on securing clear title to the thirty-three hundred acres as agreed upon in December 1916. While these formal letters were traveling back and forth in bureaucratic circles, the Army acted.

Indians were ordered to leave their homes and not return until they were given permission to do so. Some families left but many stayed, and they were simply loaded on wagons with some of their household goods and transported away from the area. A number of Indian families were given just a few hours' notice before the Army arrived to move them, and some of the people spent the remaining months of the winter in makeshift shacks along the Nisqually River wondering why the Bureau of Indian Affairs could not stop the confiscation of their homes and lands. But with the high state of excitement then prevailing in Tacoma the Indians were afraid that they would be accused of disloyalty if they complained, and so many of them simply left the reservation without saying anything.

Early in 1918, without the knowledge of the Bureau of Indian Affairs, the authorities of Pierce County began condemnation proceedings against the Nisqually lands on the north of the river, which were the best part of the reservation. When the Interior Department discovered what was happening, officials lodged a protest, albeit not a very strong one, and the Army agreed to purchase the lands from the Indians. The War Department appointed an appraiser and urged the Bureau of Indian Affairs to do the same. The bureau appointed the head of the Cushman School, an educator, as their representative, and very shortly the two appraisals were forwarded to officials in each department in the nation's capital. The War Department representative valued the lands at $57,920.60, while the Bureau of Indian Affairs representative figured the lands were worth $93,760.

In April 1918 a compromise figure was worked out that totaled $75,840, and a decree was entered by the local court vesting title in the lands to Pierce County. The legality of the transaction was not questioned, because of the hysterical fear that raising such questions might be regarded as treason in view of the war. The Army in effect purchased the Nisqually land long after it had removed the Indian owners, by allowing a local court to transfer the land titles to Pierce County, which in turn was bound by agreement to cede the Army seventy thousand acres in return for the construction of a fort near Tacoma. At best, it was a shadowy transaction, unworthy of the United States Government, but, under the circumstances, not unlikely.

The Indian agent soothed his conscience by the thought that if the transaction was illegal Congress would find some way to compensate the Nisquallies after the war. The agent was partly correct, because the controversy over the confiscation of the Nisqually reservation refused to die, and in the 1919 Indian Appropriations Act a section was inserted requiring the Secretaries of War and of the Interior to report to Congress on the advisability of reacquiring the lands of the Nisquallies from Pierce County. Apparently Congress did not believe the official War Department version of how the lands for Fort Lewis were acquired and wanted some joint statement from the two government departments on what had transpired.

So a special investigating commission was sent out to Tacoma to learn what had happened two years before, in the hysteria of war fever. In the spring of 1920 the report was finally filed with the House of Representatives Committee on Indian Affairs. Even the official version did not do credit to the United States. The report was purged of accounts of Indian families dispossessed of their homes in midwinter, but it still contained enough material to shame the two departments for their roles in the confiscation of the Indian lands.

The two department representatives first advised against restoring the lands to the Nisquallies under the theory that they were now comfortable in their new homes. Where they received such information is questionable, since the report does not indicate that they talked with very many of the Indians who had been forced to move. The second outstanding feature of the report is the acknowledgment by the two representatives that the Indians did not receive fair value for their lands regardless of how they were appraised. One white man owned land adjoining the reservation—land not nearly as good as the Nisquallies'. He received over thirty-two thousand dollars for 1,350 acres that had no river bottom lands or running water to make the land valuable.

Most puzzling was the response of the county attorneys when asked about the transaction. The investigators asked Mr. J. T. S. Lyle, one of the attorneys for Pierce County, for a copy of the Army's deed to the lands. The attorney refused to give a copy of the deed to the investigators, and when they inquired at the county offices they were informed that the deed had never been filed! The county assessor did inform the commission that had he been allowed to value these lands for tax purposes he would have appraised them at $66,650, and the commission noted that county assessors are notoriously generous when appraising lands for tax purposes.

Perhaps the best indication of how badly the Nisquallies were cheated is the condition in which they found themselves when they tried to purchase lands for new homes on the river after they had been paid for their old allotments. Willie Frank, for example, had an allotment of 205 acres on the northern side of the river which was taken for the Army post. With the money he received for the lands he was able to purchase only six and a half acres on the south bank of the river! Other Indians found themselves in similar circumstances, and many simply moved away to live on other reservations where they had relatives.

The investigators finally recommended that Congress appropriate another eighty-five thousand dollars to be paid to the Nisquallies as additional compensation for their lands. The legality of the whole transaction, dubious at best, was never mentioned. The only comment made in the report to Congress regarding the justice of the proceedings noted

that owing to war-time conditions and influences the county attorneys at the time of the condemnation proceedings took the fullest advantage of the situation, with the result that the Indians received considerably less than their lands were worth, and have not been provided with lands of like character and location and of equal advantage and acreage.

Although the investigation clearly showed that the Nisquallies did not lose their fishing rights in the condemnation proceedings, the state began harassing the Nisqually fishermen following the confiscation of their reservation on the theory that they had lost everything when the county received the lands. The Nisquallies and the state fish and game departments began an undeclared war over fishing rights that has lasted until the present time, with the Indians continually complaining that if the state officials really knew the history of their tribe they would see the justice of the Indian cause.

We shall return to the fishing-rights controversy and the Nisquallies later, because their story, far from ending, is continuing today in more heroic terms than ever before. We need only note that the suspicions of Leschi, the great Nisqually chief, about the intentions of the white settlers were unfortunately fulfilled nearly two generations after his valiant effort to achieve justice for his people, and it is tragic to note that the lands he secured with his life were taken from his people under the guise of patriotism in a wholly unnecessary act.

chapter

ELEVEN

Nor all the Indian stories in the Pacific Northwest have been as grim as those of the Puyallups and Nisquallies. Some of the tribes, such as the Makahs and the Quinaults of the coastal region of the Olympic Peninsula lived in relative isolation from the growing cities of Puget Sound and had very few intrusions by non-Indians. Other tribes, such as the Lummis and the Swinomish of the Georgia Straits region, seemed destined to survive as communities even though they had a difficult time of it.

The Lummis, who traditionally lived around Bellingham Bay and the San Juan Islands, in the northern portion of the inland waters, have a unique history and one that is, in a very important way, representative of many Indian tribes. We have met them briefly already at the negotiations during the treaty of Point Elliott and in the *Alaska Packers' Association* lawsuit in which they lost their fishing rights through no fault of their own. But let us go back for a moment to see how they fared after the treaty of Point Elliott.

Of all the villages that attended the treaty at Mucklteoh, or Point Elliott, no villages were better represented than the Lummi villages of the Bellingham area. At least a dozen chiefs and headmen attended the proceedings and signed the treaty. It was perhaps due to the size of their delegation that the Lummis secured a reservation in the heart of their ancestral lands on the island of Chah-choo-sen, where the Nooksack River splits and sends two branches into the inland waters—at Lummi Bay and at Bellingham Bay. The Lummi homelands remained relatively unknown during the fur-trading period, because the largest trading center was at Fort Langley, on Vancouver Island, and the avenues of trade bypassed the Lummis. In 1852, a couple of years before the treaty with Isaac Stevens, two white men had arrived in the area and set up a sawmill on Whatcom Creek, several miles from the largest Lummi village. The area, while attractive, was no better or worse than other places closer to the larger settlements, and the prospect of development remained remote in the years following the treaty.

But in 1858 gold was discovered in British Columbia, and in a sudden rush thousands of miners passed through the Bellingham area in search of the goldfields of Canada. The little settlement of Whatcom became a leading center for outfitting the miners, and the Lummis shared in the prosperity of the gold rush. Unfortunately they had no more foresight than did the whites at Whatcom, and in the summer of 1858 they sold all their canoes at high prices to the miners wishing to canoe up the Nooksack to British Columbia. By the end of the rush the white settlement at Whatcom had grown tremendously and the Lummis were back building canoes for the coming season's fishing, richer, somewhat wiser, and certainly swearing never again to sell every canoe, no matter what the prices.

Even though coal was discovered in paying quantities in the Bellingham area, settlement did not grow as fast as in other parts of the territory, and the Lummis and their white neighbors settled down to a life of comparative ease. The Bureau of Indian Affairs supervised the Lummis and provided schooling for them through a contract with Father Chirouse, a Catholic missionary who established a school on the nearby Tulalip reservation; for a period of twenty-one years this school was the only one available to the children of the Lummi tribe.

Finally a day school was established at Lummi, and they received a resident farmer to help them with their farming activities. Like many other government employees, the two people assigned to the Lummis were determined to carry out their program of civilization even though the circumstances at Lummi made the feasibility of any profound transformation impossible. The reservation was covered with a thick growth of cedar, and when the agent surveyed it into allotments and began his farming program problems began to pile up rapidly. The men were recruited to cut and burn the trees, some of them the finest cedar in the country, so that the land would be clear for farming. But since the land was really an island, clearing the trees resulted in the creation of many swamps and pools of almost perpetual duration. While the agents gave an optimistic report on farming at Lummi every year, listing, as we have seen on other reservations, bushels of wheat, corn, and other crops, it was apparent from the first that farming was not an occupation that would be very profitable on the reservation.

The Lummis had to seek other work from the very beginning, because their farming ventures simply proved impossi-

135

ble, and very shortly they were working in lumber camps, serving as day laborers, fishing commercially, mining coal, and working on the steamboats that traveled up and down Puget Sound. It was the Lummis who first discovered hop-picking and made it into an annual tribal event by taking friends and relatives north to British Columbia to work in the hop fields. Early newspapers recount the astonishment of the people of the area at the sight of the whole tribe embarking on a six weeks' trip to the hop fields, taking small children, old people, and invited guests with them.

The fishing activities were severely hampered, as we have seen, in the 1890s, when the U.S attorney failed to take the *Alaska Packers' Association* case to the Supreme Court, where the Lummis would almost certainly have had their rights upheld. But while they were restricted in their fishing at Point Roberts and other sites some distance from the reservation, they maintained fishing sites in the neighborhood and continued to fish as they always had. In a classic understatement of the situation at Lummi, the commissioner of Indian affairs reported in 1895:

> The Indians, as a rule, are not systematic farmers. Farming is with them the incident and not the business of everyday life. Some of them, the more thrifty and industrious, have well-cultivated farms and comfortable houses, and are anxious to have their children educated. They generally live like white people. Those, however, are the exception. A large majority spend most of their time in their canoes, fishing, especially during the salmon season.

The commissioner might have admitted to himself, and warned future commissioners, that the program to turn the Lummis into farmers was probably not going to work. Following the *Alaska Packers' Association* case, state officials seemed to concentrate their efforts to enforce the state fish laws on the Lummis rather than any other tribe, and incidents began to multiply involving the Lummis and the state fish wardens. The Bureau of Indian Affairs, while it dodged controversial incidents, generally tried to support the Lummi efforts to maintain fishing sites. But their efforts generally backfired because of the weakhearted support they gave the Lummi fishermen.

In 1913, for example, the agent at the Lummi reservation and the state fish commissioner made an agreement to have a test of the Lummi treaty fishing rights, and Harry Price, a Lummi, agreed to be arrested by the state fish commissioner so that the state supreme court or federal district court could make a definite pronouncement whether or not the Lummis had a right to fish free of state regulation. Price was arrested and the case began to travel through the courts, with the state fish commissioner confident that he would be vindicated in his contention that the state had the right to regulate the Lummi fishermen.

The Lummis won the case, and the infuriated fish commissioner refused to abide by the decision, announcing that he would continue to arrest Lummi fishermen, thus inciting a massive protest by the tribes of upper Puget Sound, who had followed the case with great interest. The large-scale Indian protest scared the federal officials, who promptly made themselves scarce, feeling that it would be unpopular to carry out their duties to protect the Indians as required by the treaties. Whatcom County, where the Lummi reservation was situated, was in an uproar, and the situation grew tense. No one knew what the Indians would do next.

But the Lummis were supremely confident, now that their federal protectors had fled the scene, and they instructed their lawyer to seek a permanent injunction against the state fish commissioner, forbidding him from arresting any Lummi fishermen. The Bellingham *Herald*, the county's most vocal newspaper, was disgusted at the whole affair, a little astounded that the Indians knew enough about the white man's law to use it effectively, and announced:

> at least it will force Commissioner Darwin to come into court and file informations to which demurrers can be taken, something which, the petition recites, he has heretofore refused to do.

Instead of proving that the Indians were violating the law, Commissioner Darwin had been arresting the Lummis and failing to show that they were violating any law, but in the process of arresting them he was confiscating their canoes and fishing gear, thus preventing them from fishing.

Darwin escaped the injunction through the co-operation of the federal officials and continued his harassment of the Lummis. But his determination to prevent the Lummis from fishing led to a very serious and, in some respects humorous, situation two years later. Some Austrian fishermen arrived in Lummi waters in 1915 on a fishing trip. (Actually they were simply fishermen on a ship flying the Austrian flag, making them, in a technical legal sense Austrian citizens, even though Austria is landlocked and has no fishing fleet.)

The Lummis, seeing this strange ship in their waters, refused to allow them to fish, and Darwin and other state officials supported the Austrians. The U.S. attorney, who was supposed to defend the Lummis, also took the side of the Austrians, and the situation looked very suspicious indeed. Both state and federal officials argued that the Lummi fishing rights extended only to the high tide and that other people were allowed to fish in the waters that bordered the reservation.

When the Indians became convinced that they would not receive any assistance from either state or federal officials, they promptly got into their canoes and paddled out to the Austrian ship and arrested the Austrians and took them back to the reservation as prisoners. With their newly acquired prisoners hidden in one of the Indian homes, the Lummis sat back to watch the proceedings.

Telephone lines hummed between Washington, D.C., Seattle, and Bellingham, and before the day was over officials in a very high position in the nation's capital were trying to explain to the President and other assorted officials why a boatload of Austrian fishermen were being held captive by the Lummi Indians. With the First World War just beginning in Europe, it was the last kind of incident that the United States wanted to happen. Dr. Charles Buchanan, the Indian agent at the Tulalip reservation, was sent on a delicate mission to negotiate with the Lummis, while other federal officials received a blistering reprimand for letting things get out of hand. Buchanan secured the release of the Austrians after hearing the Lummi side of the story, and when the full story became public the state fish commissioner decided to stop his harassment of the Lummis. Very promptly.

Events took a strange turn for the Lummis after they won their battle with the state fish commissioner, and they found themselves confronted with a prolonged attack on their lands. In 1873 the President had set aside their reservation with carefully described boundaries, and the reservation as defined in the order signed by the President gave them slightly more land than the treaty had provided.

The lands had been allotted to individual tribe members in 1885, and over the years some of the lands had been sold, leaving a pattern of Indian landholdings that resembled a checkerboard, with Indians owning some tracts of lands and non-Indians owning others. Prominent businessmen in Bellingham had purchased some of the allotments that bordered the tidelands, and in 1919, led by a man named Romaine, they claimed ownership of the tidelands, and the resulting clamor led to a lawsuit by the United States to clarify who owned the tidelands. It seemed to be a ridiculous controversy at the time, because the tidelands are that part of the shore covered by the motion of high and low tides—in other words, simply a stretch of beach that we see when the tide is out. In that stretch of beach, however, are the clams and other shellfish, which are very tasty and very valuable.

The court ruled that the Lummi reservation covered not only the lands allotted to the tribe but also the shoreline down to the low-tide line. The businessmen of Bellingham were disappointed, of course, because the Lummi beaches were beautiful and ideal spots for summer cottages, and there had been a lot of discussion of getting contol of the shore properties and developing recreation areas on the reservation.

The beach issue did not remain quiet for very long. Eleven years later, when even more Indian lands had been sold, a man named Stotts purchased an Indian allotment on the shore and claimed that his property went into the water and included the beach and waterfront. The case again went to court, and the question was whether the shoreline belonged to the tribe or to the individual property owners. The Lummis claimed that the presidential order establishing the reservation gave the shoreline to the tribe and not to individuals who later received allotments.

Again the court ruled that the Lummi tribe and not individual property owners held the title to the shoreline. It would have seemed that there were no more questions to be determined regarding the Lummi beach, but the following year one of the owners, a man named Boynton, claimed that the shifting of the shoreline in the time since the reservation was established had given him a section of beach because the water had intruded into his property lines. So the Lummis were back in court to protect their beach, and once again the court found in their favor. Even though the beach line may vary from time to time according to the height of water, the court ruled, the ownership of beach follows the water, and property lines have to give way to the general ownership of the beach.

Perhaps the most spectacular aspect of the *Boynton* case was the testimony of an old Lummi who had worked on the original survey of the reservation boundary in 1873. The old gentleman came into court hardly able to speak English and recalled almost precisely how the original federal surveyor, fifty-eight years earlier, had walked over the wilds of the reservation setting survey stakes and determining where the reservation boundaries were. When he was able to go to precisely the same locations nearly six decades later and point out the markers and places designated on the reservation map, it was no contest, and the judge ruled in favor of the tribe.

The Lummis were far from preserving their reservation lands, however, because the reservation had been divided up into little farming tracts of forty acres, and over the years much of the land was sold by individual Indians. As each piece of land left Indian hands, the reservation grew smaller and the people received less attention from the Bureau of Indian Affairs, who argued that their job was only to protect the Indian lands, not to provide services to the people who lived on the lands. Although this attitude was in direct conflict with the treaty at Point Elliott, the Lummis were helpless to prevent the government from withdrawing its services from them.

After 1931, when the *Boynton* case was decided in their favor, until 1968, when the tribe began to get aggressive about protecting its lands, the Lummis suffered a general decline in their fortunes. The government day school was closed, and the children were sent to local white schools off the reservation, where they were not welcomed. Land speculators continued to pressure the Bureau of Indian Affairs to sell the Lummi lands to them, because the lands were becoming increasingly valuable as recreation properties. Finally, by 1968, there was only one tract of land in the whole reservation that bordered the shore, and it was owned by a prominent Lummi family. All the other shoreland had been sold over the years. While the tribe still owned the beach and the people still dug clams, there was profound gloom among the Lummis that with the sale of this final piece of land they would no longer have any way to get to the beach.

In 1967 the Lummis suddenly discovered that plans were under way to locate a magnesium-oxide reduction plant on Lummi Bay. The plans were to bring the raw ore into the bay by ship and use the fresh water of Lummi Bay in the reduction process. The raw ore was a deep-green, olivine color and, once processed, would produce tremendous heaps of waste that would permanently destroy all marine life in the bay. The people were terrified at the thought of destroying the bay, but they seemed to have no choice. The large corporate and banking interests were eager to have the new industry, and even many of the white people in the county saw the new plant as a means of developing the county.

About a week before they had to make the final decision whether to accept the ore-reduction plant, the Lummis encountered Dr. Wallace Heath, a marine biologist who was interested in aquaculture, the scientific farming of seafood such as salmon, clams, and oysters. When Heath discovered that

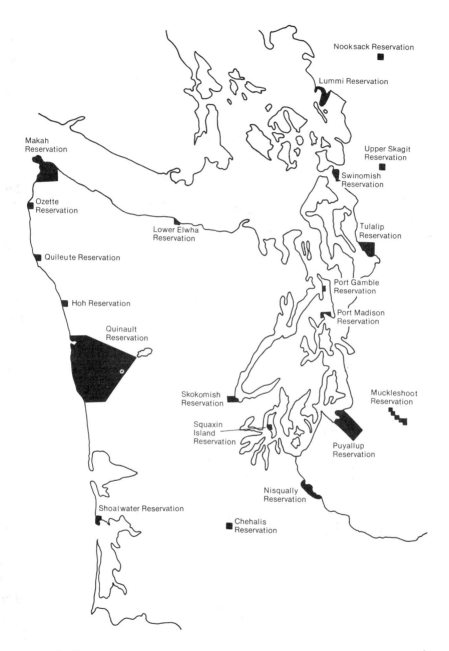

Indian reservations in Washington State at the present time.

the tribe was just about to approve the ore-reduction plant, he became concerned, being an ecologist, that the plant would destroy surrounding fish life in the neighboring bays, and he agreed to visit Lummi Bay and give a professional opinion on whether or not the new plant would hurt the fisheries that provided the only continuing source of income to the Lummis.

Heath and the Lummi leaders toured the bay and took samples of the water in various parts of the area. Heath announced that the bay showed great potential for the development of an aquaculture, even though the idea was very new and few people had tried to build a successful aquaculture. When the Lummi discovered what was required for an aquaculture, they surely must have smiled at the irony of history. An aquaculture needs that stretch of beach between high and low tide and depends, in a freshwater bay, on the action of the tides to provide movement and fresh water every day. And the stretch of beach between high and low tide was the only thing left in the original reservation that still belonged to the tribe!

We will discuss the Lummi aquaculture in a later chapter, because it is one of the most unique experiments ever undertaken by a tribe of Indians. But it is comforting to learn that while many of the other tribes in the Pacific Northwest lost their beloved homelands in strange and unjust ways, the Lummis somehow were able to save precisely that part of their ancestral lands that was most valuable. There may be a force in history that sometimes compensates for the tragic experiences of people.

chapter
TWELVE

THE twentieth century brought many changes in the lives of the Indians of the Pacific Northwest, but perhaps the most profound change was the gradual settlement of the region and the erosion of concern shown by the federal government for the various reservations. While the state was unsettled and large stretches of territory had few residents, there seemed to be a great need for special government schools and services for Indians. But gradually more and more towns and cities grew up, some at the expense of the tribes, as we have seen in the case of Tacoma, which took the lands of the Puyallups and Nisquallies in two separate incidents.

With the increased settlement in Washington State there was a decrease in the number of services provided by the federal government to the tribes. Perhaps the first tangible indication of the change was the closing of the different reservation day schools. These reservations had each received a government school and a teacher, and for nearly a generation they had enjoyed the benefits of an elementary education at their homes. As local educational programs expanded, government officials began to question the great expense of the reservation day schools. They argued, and quite persuasively, that since the Indians and the whites worked and played together, there was no reason why they should not be educated together.

So, over a twenty-year period beginning about 1900, the day schools on the reservations were closed. The various reservation governments reacted in various ways. Some of the people wished to have their children in the local school systems, because they felt that the children would receive a better education than they were getting in the government schools. But other Indians felt that the government had intended to provide special schooling for their children under the treaties made by Isaac Stevens and so they saw the closing of the schools as another indication of the government's going back on its word.

With the closing of the schools came a general reduction in the number of government employees on each reservation. No longer did the government provide a boss farmer to supervise the farming activities of the Indians, and the Indian police, who had been so effective in helping to govern the reservations and protect the people from intruders, were also eliminated, leaving many reservations without any police protection at all.

But it was becoming more difficult for the federal government to provide services to the various reservations because of the very technical problems that began to arise regarding their lands. When the reservations were established, it was clear that all the lands were held by the federal government in a trust for the tribes who lived on the reservations and that federal laws would be applied to those who committed illegal acts on the Indian lands. As the individual allotments were sold by Indians and purchased by non-Indians, the lands themselves became taxable, because they were no longer held by the federal government. And state officials began to argue that if they were taxing the lands inside the reservations they should have the power to enforce state laws inside the reservations also.

This very complicated problem became known as "jurisdiction." Who had the authority to enforce the rules of law on the reservations? Whenever it was convenient for the state to claim the authority, state officials would assert themselves, and whenever it was convenient for federal officials to claim their privileges, they would do so. We have already seen that when neither the state nor the federal officials exerted themselves, the Indians claimed their own authority, as the Lummis did in the arrest of the Austrian fishermen.

The jurisdiction problem was only one of the problems that arose with the withdrawal of local Bureau of Indian Affairs agents from the reservations. The state fish and game departments were unusually energetic about enforcing the laws against the Indians, and without a local representative of the Bureau of Indian Affairs to speak up for them many Indians were arrested for fishing under the provisions of the treaties. Practically all the tribes continued their traditional fishing activities, and the loss of land and confusion over jurisdiction created great hardships for them.

When the commission was sent out to investigate the situation of the Nisquallies, the first thing they learned was that the confiscation of the riverbank lands had led to great hardships, because the Nisquallies could no longer fish for their food and had so small an income from their other activities that they could not feed themselves. Father DeDecker, the local Catholic missionary to the Nisquallies, told the commission, "this fishing privilege was the most valuable right they lost by being dispossessed of their lands." "Their main dependence for meat was fish," Father DeDecker related, "secured by them from the Nisqually River where it passes through the reservation where they fished unmolested and dried large quantities of salmon for winter use."

The Nisquallies were similar to many tribes in their daily diet during these years. Their meals generally consisted of bread, potatoes, and salmon, which they either boiled, barbecued, or baked. Quite often, the poorer Indian families lacked money for potatoes and bread after they lost their lands, and salmon was the only dish served. "Most of the Nisqually Indians ate fish daily," Father DeDecker told the investigating commission; "in fact, if deprived of fish some of them would have nearly starved." It was the same with the other tribes.

It might not have been so hard on the Indians to have their fishing regulated had it not been for the dreadful conservation practices of the white farmers in the area. They saw only a land of plenty and apparently thought that the salmon were inexhaustible, for they took no care to see that the fish were used wisely. An old settler in the Puyallup Valley who spent his whole life near the Puyallup reservation described the common practice of the new farmers to use the salmon for fertilizer in their fields:

At the headwaters of a short creek emptying into the Puyallup River, which in turn in a few miles poured its accumulated water into the tide water of Puget Sound, I have seen the salmon so numerous on the shoal water of the channel as to literally touch each other. It was utterly impossible to wade across without touching the fish.

At certain seasons I have sent my team, accompanied by two armed men with pitchforks, to load up from the riffle for fertilizing the hop fields.

If we remember the very careful ceremony of the first salmon, which the tribes held with the first run of the fish to ensure the continual return of the salmon to the river, we can understand the heartbreak and resentment felt by the Indians who were being arrested for fishing while the white farmers were carelessly wasting the fish by using them for fertilizer.

Seeing these great injustices, the Indians organized to fight back, and over the years a number of organizations were created to bring the tribes together in a common fight against the fish and game departments. The result of these frequent clashes was that the state departments would often relax their efforts to arrest the Indian fishermen until a court case could be initiated that, everyone hoped, would settle the question once and for all. The state attorneys almost always attacked the treaty clause that gave the Indians the right to fish "in common" with the other citizens, claiming that the treaty only gave the Indians the same rights as everyone else. While the state might win the first hearing of the case in a state court, which viewed the arguments sympathetically, the state would lose when the case was appealed to the federal court, which normally followed the Indian understanding of the treaty.

But the Indians were not always successful in the federal courts. One of the most important movements in the 1920s saw all the tribes of the Point Elliott treaty area band together in a large claims suit against the government for failure to fulfill the treaty requirements. In those days the idea of Indians suing the United States for failure to fulfill treaty obligations was a very new thing, and the tribes had to secure a special law from Congress in order to file their suit. The story of the tribes of the Pacific Northwest was well known in Congress, and it was hoped that the suit would settle all the questions concerning the treaty.

The case was finally decided in 1936, and the Indians did not receive any money for the loss of their lands. If the case did anything, it illustrated how differently the Indian and the white man had always looked at lands and ways of living. The court felt that the treaty was really just a contract to sell a tract of land and interpreted the document accordingly, insisting on the literal interpretation of the various words and phrases. The Indians understood the oral tradition their fathers and grandfathers had passed down by word of mouth, and this tradition consisted of the promises Isaac Stevens had made that were by and large not recorded on paper at the time he spoke. The case was one of the first in which a group of Indians had gotten an opportunity to present their arguments. As a result there was great confusion among the experts for both the Indians and the government about what documents and testimony really were essential to determine the meaning of the treaty. It was a mistake that the Indians would remember a generation later.

A happier note on treaties was recorded early in the twentieth century, when the descendants of the Chinooks on the Pacific Coast were able to get a Congressional committee to review the old treaties signed by their grandfathers and Anson Dart. In 1906 the Secretary of the Interior was authorized to send an investigating committee to Oregon and Washington in order to interview the remaining Chinooks and determine how many people still lived in their old homelands. A considerable number were found, and the Congress made a special appropriation to compensate them for the failure of the United States to ratify their treaties.

Shortly after the Lower Chinooks received their payments on the 1851 treaties their northern cousins who lived along the beaches of Washington were given allotments on the Quinault reservation in that state. The original reservation had been very small, because the Chinooks and the Cowlitz and other small villages had refused to sign a treaty with Isaac Stevens, and so there was no need to give the Quinaults and Quileutes, who had signed a treaty, a large reservation. But about thirty years after Stevens signed the treaty, at a time when the Bureau of Indian Affairs was busy establishing reservations and failing to notify its local agents, the Quinault reservation was greatly expanded, and Indian agents were ordered to encourage other tribes to settle at Taholah, the headquarters of the Quinault reservation. It was not until the 1920s that any serious movement rose to take up lands on the reservation, and many of the people from the scattered bands simply accepted allotments at Quinault and continued to live in the small beach communities where they had traditionally lived.

When the Great Depression swept across the country, the Indians of the Pacific Northwest reservations fared much better than their white neighbors. They had been used to living under the simplest of conditions, and fish had always been the mainstay of their diet. It was no hardship on them to live in the isolated reservation communities and continue to fish and dig clams. In fact the government programs that were created as part of the New Deal effort to provide employment for the millions of Americans who were out of work proved quite compatible to the Indians of the Pacific Northwest. The most popular program was the Civilian Conservation Corps, and camps were set up on some of the reservations. Since the government could not refuse local Indians a chance to participate in the program, many Indians joined the C.C.C., and for the first time in reservation history, a steady employment program was made available to reservation residents.

Of much more importance during the depression years was the startling reversal of federal Indian policy. Ever since the reservations were established, the official policy had been to teach the Indians agriculture and ensure their eventual assimilation into local society. As we have seen, the constant intrusions of settlers on the reservations led to the creation of reservation councils and Indian police forces and eventually to the appointment of local Indian judges to govern the Indian communities. Thus while the official policy was to stifle Indian self-government, in practice the Indian agent had no alternative but to help the Indians develop their own governments.

After the turn of the century the reduction of government employees meant a decline in the fortunes of reservation governments also. While the tribes had a local Indian agent, it was fairly easy to get his daily opinion on how things should operate, and people showed a great interest in developing their communities. But with the reservations lacking agents and decisions being made in remote places under the various consolidations that were taking place in the Bureau of Indian Affairs, people lost interest in reservation affairs and drifted away.

In 1934 President Roosevelt and Indian Commissioner John Collier formulated a new Indian policy, which allowed the tribes to organize their reservations as federal corporations and govern the communities themselves. The law that made this policy possible was called the Indian Reorganization Act, or, more popularly, the Wheeler-Howard Act, after Senator Wheeler of Montana and Representative Howard, who sponsored the legislation.

A number of the smaller reservations accepted the Indian

Reorganization Act and organized tribal governments under its provisions. The best part of the act was the provision that the Secretary of the Interior could purchase lands and give them to the tribes that had lost out during the previous decades, when it was federal policy to sell Indian lands. Although many of the smaller groups saw this provision as the best argument for accepting the act, they were to be disappointed. The intent of Congress had been to purchase lands for Indians in those parts of the country where lands were selling very cheaply and to restore those lands. When the policy was applied in the state of Washington, people quickly noted that the lands that could be purchased to add to the reservation holdings were very expensive, in some cases the acquisition of waterfront properties and other badly needed tracts of land costing more than the Bureau of Indian Affairs was able or willing to spend. In addition, local whites who were being forced to sell their lands because of difficult financial problems did not take kindly to having the government purchase their lands and give them to the Indians.

The Indians of the Pacific Northwest did not really benefit from the provisions of the Indian Reorganization Act as other tribes in the nation did. In fact the act probably confused their legal status even more. The tribes who developed constitutions under the act were supposed to receive the same powers of self-government as the larger tribes in other states. But when the government refused to provide them with land over which they could govern, it created a difficult situation, in which the tribal councils had all the powers of a state of the union but very tiny parcels of land over which to exercise these powers.

In spite of the difficulties in developing new governments many of the reservations made great strides in the years before the Second World War. Local industries were started, and fishing activities increased tremendously, with some tribes starting small tribal fish markets where the Indian fishermen could sell their fish at a better price than they would have received from the local fish buyers. Different types of activities were started to raise funds for the tribal governments. Some tribes sold tribal fishing and hunting permits to outsiders to raise funds. When tribal courts were established, the income from fines levied in these courts were made available to the tribal governments. And probably most important, the developing community spirit of the reservations led to the establishment of fairs and powwows, which were used to raise money.

The Indian Reorganization Act allowed freedom of religion on the reservations for the first time since they were established. The first Indian agents had banned most of the old ceremonies, and the Indians had had to hold their most sacred ceremonies in secret or, as we have seen, under the pretense of celebrating the Fourth of July or other holidays celebrated by the whites.

Perhaps the biggest change before the Second World War was in education. People in the Bureau of Indian Affairs had always believed that Indians were good at working with their hands but that they could not be educated to perform administrative tasks that required a formal knowledge of American institutions. The Indian Reorganization Act gave Indians preference in employment in the Bureau of Indian Affairs, and it allowed tribes to give loans to their members for educational purposes. With this official encouragement, many Indians of the Pacific Northwest began to attend college. Others sought employment in the Bureau of Indian Affairs and began to work their way up in the civil service. For the first time in history the horizons of the people were raised above the local level, and they began to understand how the rest of the world lived and worked.

The Second World War practically devastated the Indian programs all across the nation. There were few government funds available to be spent on Indians, because of the war effort, and since many of the people moved to the cities to do war work and most of the young men joined the armed forces, the reservations appeared to be practically deserted. The only thing that the Bureau of Indian Affairs could do was to encourage Indians to participate in the war effort and keep a skeleton force working to sell lands and arrange timber leases. Victory gardens were encouraged, and Indian fishermen were not bothered, because they were busy providing food for the people as they had been for nearly a century and a half. The victory-garden project was so successful that bureau employees tried to continue it after the war.

Following the war, when the Indian veterans returned to the reservations, they started many changes. One of the first things they did was to enter into community life and try to get the tribal governments back on the road to development which they had begun before the war. Almost every reservation had its local post of the American Legion or the Veterans of Foreign Wars, and these Indian posts took an active part in community development, sponsoring scout troops, youth programs, community fund-raising projects, and beautification programs. Many of the Indian veterans had seen foreign countries and believed that they could build the reservations up the way other peoples were now building up their communities.

Eligibility for veterans' benefits enabled many of the Indian vets to start small businesses; fishing was the most popular. Before the war few Indians had done more than fish in their traditional manner with a canoe or nets. Now they began to purchase deepwater boats that could compete with non-Indian fishermen in large catches. By the end of the 1940s dozens of Indians were in commercial fishing, thanks to loans from their veterans benefits, and long voyages along the seacoast to Alaska and California to catch salmon and tuna were not uncommon.

By the 1950s most Indians lived in the same manner as did the whites of the area. Most of them had moved away from their reservations and now held industrial jobs in the cities or in small towns, particularly in airplane manufacturing, a major industry in Washington State. The few people living on the reservations mostly fished or ran small farms, and remained very traditional in their attitudes toward life. They continued many of the customs of their ancestors and looked with some suspicion at the Indians who had moved away from the reservations.

The people who lived in the large cities, while they did have jobs and were determined to make a success of their new lives as city dwellers, developed a great nostalgia for the reservation. They missed the community gatherings and the slower and friendlier way of living on the reservations. In the cities it was difficult for relatives to visit them, and with jobs they often had to miss the old celebrations they had enjoyed at home. To cure their loneliness they traveled home as often as possible and often visited other reservations for celebrations in order to enjoy the few hours of Indian life they provided. The result of such extensive visiting was that the Indians got to know each other again, and the isolation that the different reservations had often felt in the old days gradually faded as they were able to travel. In many ways the Indians went back to their prewhite days, when people spent a great deal of time traveling back and forth visiting.

In the 1950s the salmon catches began to decline rapidly. There was little realistic control over the fishing industry, and the new techniques for catching fish meant that there were fewer and fewer fish returning to the spawning grounds each year. Like a ghost out of the past the old controversy over fishing rights began to heat up again. By the mid-fifties the Indian commercial fishermen could no longer compete in the deep waters because of the cost of fishing boats. A good fishing boat cost about $125,000, and even with a series of good seasons behind him an Indian fisherman simply did not have the income to purchase the better equipment, so most of the Indians returned to their canoes and nets along the rivers.

With an increasing number of Indians now fishing in their traditional river sites the state fish and game wardens became determined to gain jurisdiction over Indian fishing. They claimed that the Indians were ruining their conservation programs by fishing on the traditional fishing grounds without supervision. In 1947 the state legislature had designated the steelhead trout as a game fish, and this meant that it could not be sold commercially, like salmon. There was little controversy at first over the designation, but as more and more white sportsmen began fishing for steelhead and more Indians were forced to return to the rivers, serious conflicts broke out.

The states of Washington, Idaho, and Oregon made a concentrated effort to force Indians to purchase state fishing licenses, and arrests were made of Indians for fishing without state licenses. When these cases began to be decided by the higher state and federal courts, the old arguments over the phrase "fishing in common with other citizens" became the most hotly debated words since "fifty-four forty or fight." By the beginning of the 1960s the Indians were determined to fight to the death for fishing rights, and since they were so

A sixty-pound salmon caught in a tribal fish trap by a member of the Swinomish tribe, 1938.

scattered around the Puget Sound area and shared so many things in common, fishing became the great issue on which all Indians agreed.

Sentiment gathered rapidly in the late 1950s as the Indians watched the civil rights movement make impressive gains in the South. Younger Indians began to speak out at Indian meetings urging the older people to engage in similar protest movements to clarify the treaty rights once and for all. Since everything was moving toward a general Indian protest in the Pacific Northwest, the actions of the game wardens only fueled the fires of resentment that were burning among the Indians. In the next chapter we shall see how the "fish-in" came about and what that accomplished. It is enough here to note that the idea of self-government, which had been planted in the depression years and had always been alive among the people since before the coming of the Americans, was now a mature idea in the minds of the Indians of the Puget Sound area.

chapter THIRTEEN

As we have seen previously, there seemed to be continuous conflict between state officials in the Fish and Game department and the Indians of the various reservations over fishing rights. It was almost a standard rule that Indians would lose in the state courts but would win when they appealed their case to higher, federal courts. Thus it was that state officers devised a special strategy for dealing with the Indian fishermen. They would arrest the fishermen and confiscate their nets, knowing that if the Indian fishermen were without their nets or boats during the short time of the salmon run on their river, the effect would be to stop Indian fishing altogether.

As the decade of the 1960s opened, more and more Indians were appealing their cases and the state had to devise a different strategy to prevent them from fishing. At first the technique was to refuse to return the confiscated fishing gear under the theory that it was forfeited to the state simply because the Indian was arrested. Since the fishing gear often cost several hundred dollars, one arrest in a fishing season would put the Indian fisherman out of business until he could find a job and save the money needed to purchase new equipment. As the Indian determination to fish grew stronger, the favorite technique was to use such brutality in making the arrest that the Indian could be charged with resisting arrest, and the charge of fishing, which the state was sure to lose, would not even have to be filed.

Tensions grew rapidly on the rivers of lower Puget Sound as more and more Indians resented the unfair tactics of the state fish and game officers; and as Indian resistance grew, the state also grew more oppressive. In October of 1963, the state obtained an injunction against the Indians to prevent them from fishing in the Green River, and in January 1964, Pierce County Superior Court issued an injunction against the Nisquallies, closing that river below the Nisqually reservation, where most of the Indians had moved following the confiscation of their reservation during the First World War.

Where other tribes might have flinched at the opponents, the Nisquallies, who had fought one war against the United States to preserve their fishing, promptly organized a group called the Survival of American Indians, dedicated to fighting any encroachments on their off-reservation fishing rights. Modeling their tactics somewhat after the civil rights movement in the South, the Indians had a "fish-in" early in 1964 to protest the actions of the state. They felt that with publicity their story could be told to the public and the state would be forced to back down and stop its attempts to get Indian fishing banned on the two rivers.

The fish-in did attract attention, and in March actor Marlon Brando, who had been active in civil rights marches in the South, arrived in Washington State to participate in a demonstration in Olympia, the state capital. Brando and a Nisqually paddled out into the river in plain sight of the state game officials and lowered a net into the river. They were promptly arrested for illegal fishing, but, as the Indians figured, this arrest created problems for the state. Every day that Brando would spend in jail would mean national publicity for the fish-in and the possibility of more people coming to help the Indians. So a legal technicality was created and the state dropped the case against Brando in an effort to escape the publicity he was bringing to the fishing-rights issue.

The organizer of the fish-in was a very talented Indian then a teen-ager, Hank Adams, an Assiniboin Indian who had grown up on the Quinault reservation on the Pacific coast of Washington. Hank moved into a leadership role in Survival of American Indians several years later and was to prove more than a match for both state and federal lawyers. In 1964, however, Hank was so young that most experienced Indians in the fishing-rights struggle did not know him; nor did they see, as he did, the need for developing contacts with policymakers in Washington, D.C., in order to get the fishing-rights problem taken seriously by federal officials. Hank went to Washington, D.C., and began visiting the offices of senators and congressmen, asking them to introduce legislation to preserve fishing rights.

Senator Warren Magnuson of Washington introduced two resolutions in the United States Senate designed to solve the fishing-rights problem. Senate Joint Resolution 170 would have recognized the Indian treaty rights, but it provided that the state could regulate the off-reservation fishing, while Senate Joint Resolution 171 would have made the United States purchase all off-reservation fishing rights for a cash settlement. Magnuson held hearings in Washington in August 1964, and members of most of the tribes of the Pacific Northwest appeared at the hearings, as did the Fish and Game departments of Washington, Idaho, and Oregon. The states, of course, were content with the idea of the federal government's purchasing the Indian fishing rights, but the Indians protested so vigorously that both resolutions were allowed to die in committee.

While the tribes of Washington, Oregon, and Idaho all had treaty fishing rights, the struggle quickly resolved itself to one between the state of Washington and the Puyallup, Nisqually, and Muckleshoot tribes over the steelhead run on the Puyallup, Nisqually, and Green rivers in February and March of each year. Other tribes in other states might get an occasional arrest by state officers, but the struggle centered in the Tacoma-Olympia area with the smallest tribes in the area. The state departments carefully avoided any confrontations with the larger tribes, such as the Yakimas, who lived east of the Cascades and kept a very capable lawyer on call to handle their problems. The Nisquallies and Puyallups had no lawyers and no funds for lawyers, and so they were natural victims.

In February 1965 a group of Nisquallies and Puyallups sent a "Petition for Action" to the U. S. Attorney General asking for his assistance in a case then being conducted. They called his attention to a federal statute that reads: ". . . in all states and territories where there are reservations or allotted Indians the United States attorney shall represent them in all suits of law and in equity." But the Justice Department refused to assist the Indians, with the excuse that it had not helped them in the past in this area, even though many previous cases, including the *Winans* case, clearly indicated the opposite.

The Indians went to the state capitol at Olympia again that February, but the demonstration attracted fewer people and it appeared as if some of the Indians were getting tired of the struggle. October 1965 saw the most violent confrontation of the conflict. The Indians at Frank's Landing were fishing in the river across from Fort Lewis when a boat of game wardens attacked them and spilled them from their boat into the water. Fights broke out, and several nights later the state game officers attempted a night raid on Frank's Landing, which was federal trust property, a clear violation of federal statutes.

On October 13, the Indians announced that they would fish under their treaty, and the resulting publicity drew an unusual number of well-wishers and state officials to the landing. When the Indians put a canoe into the water, the state officers charged and a desperate battle ensued. The Indians used paddles, sticks, and stones while the state officers, outnumbering the Indians nearly five to one, had large clubs. Women and children were beaten, and the men, aware that the game wardens probably had snipers hidden in the bushes, put up a token fight, afraid of being assassinated from ambush. The Indians were arrested, and on the twenty-sixth of October the Survival of American Indians Association marched in protest at the federal courthouse in Seattle.

The following spring, Dick Gregory, the black entertainer deeply committed to human rights, arrived to assist the Survival people. He was arrested while participating in the fishins, convicted of illegal fishing, and jailed. Gregory served his sentence in the Thurston County jail, where he conducted a hunger strike. This incident gave the Indians a much needed boost in morale, for despite the fact that he was needed so badly by his own people in the South, Gregory had nonetheless come up to Washington to help the Nisquallies.

By mid-1966 the Indians, under the leadership of Hank Adams, had learned a great many things about fighting the state and federal officials. They carefully researched the status of Frank's Landing and were able to show that it was in fact a legally constituted part of the reservation under the act confiscating the Nisqually lands. They pointed out that there were about 4,500 non-Indian commercial fishermen taking about 80 per cent of the salmon in the sound and offshore before the Indians even got a chance to fish and that there were 187,525 steelhead cards issued to non-Indians and 140,375 fishermen actually out fishing. When the public saw these figures and realized that fewer than a thousand Indians fished in the whole state and not more than a couple of hundred fished the three controversial rivers, public opinion began to shift.

In March 1966 the Muckleshoot tribal council approved a fish-in designed to establish a test case. Four Muckleshoots gill-netted salmon in the Green River near Neeley's Bridge, a traditional fishing site. They were arrested and convicted in court, and appealed the case. The Indians were granted a retrial in January 1968, and the United States, which was half-heartedly trying to appear as the defender of Indian rights, hired Ms. Barbara Lane of Victoria, British Columbia, as an expert witness in anthropology to testify on the treaty rights of the Muckleshoots.

The Indians had never enjoyed the services of a scholar to help them prove their case, while the government thinking was that an anthropologist would make it seem as if the United States was fulfilling its treaty responsibilities. Federal officials, not really expecting Barbara Lane to discover anything new, were content that the Indians' accusation that they had failed to do their duty would be easily squashed.

But it turned out that Barbara Lane was a first-class scholar, who could spend endless hours in obscure research just to check a source of information. When she got on the stand in the retrial in King County Superior Court, a revolutionary change occurred in the fishing-rights struggle. Citing sources of impeccable origin, she calmly reviewed the history of the treaty and informed the court that the Muckleshoots were indeed treaty Indians and that the intent of the treaty was to preserve all traditional fishing sites for the Indians. The rest has become Indian history. Barbara Lane has been recognized as the leading authority on the Pacific Northwest Indians and has testified in numerous cases, always finding additional materials to make the Indian case even stronger.

The Indian case was hardly won, however, because the two major cases, those involving the Puyallups and the Nisquallies, had by this time reached the Supreme Court of the United States, and in June the court announced its decision. The court was unanimous in finding that the state had jurisdiction over off-reservation fishing. Justice Douglas' opinion, comparing the prosecution of Indians for off-reservation fishing to the prosecution of Indians for crime committed outside the reservation, was so confusing that even state officials complained that they did not know how to enforce the ruling. In essence, the court ruled that Indians had off-reservation rights and that the state could regulate them but not in a discriminatory manner.

The first action by the state officials was to return to Frank's Landing in an effort to test the Supreme Court decision or at least to obtain a situation in which they could get another court to expand that ruling. But the Nisquallies maintained that Frank's Landing was protected by a federal trust and that the state therefore had no right to arrest anyone there. State officers patrolled the river around Frank's Landing, and it was apparent that a confrontation was imminent. In a well-publicized "Citizen's Letter to His Governor" Hank Adams informed the governor that the Nisquallies were armed and would resist the game wardens. "The Armed Guards are under specific instructions to use weapons ONLY

State trooper holding a gun on an Indian boy during the raid on the Nisqually Indian fishing site near Tacoma, Washington, September 1970.

to prevent the specific actions by State enforcement officers to (1) trespass upon this property for the purpose of making an arrest or serving a state-issued warrant of arrest; and (2) trespassing for the purpose of confiscating the fishing net emplaced in the river off Frank's Landing and affixed to it," Adams wrote.

"If State enforcement officers attempt to proceed upon the Property of Frank's Landing after being warned against trespass," the letter continued, ". . . the weapon will be used against the trespassers. Likewise, if the net is emplaced in the water off Frank's Landing, the weapon will be used against any State officer placing a hand upon that net. . . ." "The weapon" was the one gun the Nisquallis proposed to use against the state officers. They preferred to restrict their use of arms to one identifiable weapon in order to prevent the

167

State fish and game wardens about to raid the Indian fishing site near Tacoma.

state officers from maintaining that all the Indians were using guns and giving them an excuse to shoot up the landing. A bloody confrontation was avoided when the state knew the Indians were serious.

By the fall of 1969 the state had eased off quite a bit from its former hard-line stand against the Indians. The Department of Fisheries allowed an off-reservation Nisqually fishery to exist near the reservation but carefully excluded the people at Frank's Landing in partial punishment for their resistance. But the people at Frank's Landing carried guns and fished anyway.

The big confrontation occurred the following year at a fishing camp near Tacoma on the old Puyallup reservation. A large number of Indians were fishing near a railroad bridge when they were surrounded and brutally beaten and arrested. Their cars and personal property were confiscated, and many cars were destroyed by vandalism while in police hands. The brutality against the Indians was incredible: nearly six hundred state officers participated in the "great Tacoma bust." A Chicano girl, Dolores Varela, took pictures of the police brutality and carefully hid the film when she was searched, thus providing evidence that the police had simply brutalized the Indians.

I happened to be in New York City the week after the "bust" and had an opportunity to be a guest on the Dick Cavett Show. Dick very graciously allowed me a full half hour to show pictures of the incident, some of which are reproduced in this book. The public outcry was immediate and proved a great embarrassment to the Nixon administration. Federal officials promptly announced that they had filed a major lawsuit against the state of Washington to protect the Indian treaty fishing rights but that the publicity from the Tacoma "bust" had not influenced them at all! They were

169

State game warden using a telescopic rifle from ambush during the Tacoma "bust."

planning to do so anyway, White House spokesmen asserted, and the timing was just a coincidence.

At any rate, the suit *United States* v. *Washington* was filed in federal district court in Washington. The state used its best lawyers, and the federal government had a fairly competent set of attorneys for the first time. But the Indians also had Barbara Lane as their expert witness, and by this time she knew more about the treaty than any of the lawyers on either side. The case took about three years to hear. Judge George Boldt, who heard the case, began the hearings on a note of ridicule, implying that the Indians' ability to present any rational basis for their interpretation of the treaty was remote at best. But the judge changed his mind as more evidence was presented, and in the end he found that the Indians did indeed have treaty rights to fish and suggested that an allocation of one half of the fish to the Indians might be a fair division of the resource.

While the "Boldt decision," as it is called, is very unpopular in the Pacific Northwest, it is a faithful rendering of the law based upon the best evidence made available to the court. It is doubtful if any future case on fishing rights will see such a mass of evidence put forward in support of a legal question. Under the decision, the tribal governments have the duty of policing their traditional fishing sites and of drawing up a tribal fishing code that would indicate an ability to cope with the very complex problems involved.

Perhaps the only sour note on this greatest of all Indian legal victories has been the response of the Interior Department, the people committed by federal law to act as the protector of the Indians. After the Tacoma "bust" Hank Adams discovered that the Bureau of Indian Affairs people had told the Tacoma police they had the right to arrest the Indian fishermen and, in fact, encouraged them to do whatever was necessary to prevent the Indians from fishing. The bureau hastily backtracked when the publicity of the "bust" proved so embarrassing to the government.

Following the "Boldt decision," the tribes asked for federal funds to assist them in developing tribal codes and ordinances for carrying out their responsibilities under the decision. Although nearly six hundred thousand dollars was allocated by Congress to assist the Indians in fulfilling their responsibilities as outlined by Judge Boldt, the money was very slow in coming, and Hank Adams tried to find out why the Interior Department was not carrying out its task of helping the Indians get organized. Adams discovered that the Interior officials had planned to see that the money went to Washington State agencies rather than to the tribes!

The fishing-rights struggle continues today, and headlines in the state of Washington are filled with the angry protests of sportsmen and commercial fishermen who feel that the "Boldt decision" is robbing them of income and recreation. The Indians are angry because they sincerely want to carry out a regional program of conservation and supervised fishing rights under the new responsibilities they have been given. But the Bureau of Indian Affairs, which has responsibility to help the Indians, continues to do everything in its power to prevent the tribes from acting and to foment conflict between the Indians and the sportsmen.

River net fishing has not been the only struggle of Indians in the Pacific Northwest in recent years. As part of their program to raise funds for court costs, the people at Frank's Landing began a program of selling cigarettes on their allotment. Under the Medicine Creek treaty provisions, the Indians agreed to cease their trade with Vancouver Island, and Hank Adams interpreted this phrase to mean that aside from trading with the British there were no other controls imposed on Indian commerce by the treaty. So the Nisquallies purchased cigarettes in Oregon and transported them to Washington, free of Washington State tax, for resale to anyone who would drive to the landing.

The state tax officials responded in the same manner as had the game wardens. Trucks carrying the cigarettes into the

State fish and game officers attacking Indian children during the raid.

state were confiscated and sold, while the people were harassed frequently by tax officials. The irony of the situation was that there were several military reservations in the state (including the infamous Fort Lewis) where people could purchase tax-free cigarettes, and therefore when the state argued that it should have taxing power over federal reservations, it was not simply attacking the Indians but was attempting to tax the military posts also. The military personnel found themselves being used against the Indians in the fishing-rights struggle and in the same boat with the Indians when it came to purchasing items free of state tax.

The Indians solved the problem in a very clever manner by using the giant federal bureaucracy against itself. Realizing that it was also federal law that no one could confiscate the United States mail, the people at Frank's Landing simply mailed large cartons of cigarettes to themselves to be delivered at Frank's Landing. The cigarettes were insured, of course, and the moment they were delivered at Frank's Landing they were leaving the hands of federal employees and being unloaded on federal trust property. The state had no chance to intervene in what was really an all-federal operation, and so today the Nisquallies at Frank's Landing have a nice cigarette store where they make a comfortable income with which to pay for new nets, lawyers, and other luxuries they have never had.

No one knows how long the struggle between the state of Washington and the tribes of Puget Sound will last, but it certainly seems as if the state has finally met its match in this generation of Indians. The contest was unequal for so long, with merely a handful of Indians at Frank's Landing resisting the combined powers of both the state of Washington and the United States Government, that hardly anyone gave the

State troopers handcuffing Allison Bridges, a fifteen-year-old Nisqually Indian girl.

Indians much of a chance to win. But they had a great determination that would have pleased old Chief Leschi no end, and when the smoke finally cleared they stood tall as the winners, with both state and federal people protesting that they had *always* been in favor of Indian rights.

chapter
FOURTEEN

Not all the fishing activities of the Indians of the Pacific Northwest have involved the violence and legal complications that the Nisquallies, Puyallups, and Muckleshoots have suffered. The Lummis have used their treaty rights, preserved even in the face of severe pressure by Fish Commissioner Darwin earlier in the century, and created one of the most unique experiments in the United States: an aquaculture, the scientific farming of sea food such as oysters, salmon, and trout.

You will recall that by the 1960s about all the Lummis had left of their original reservation established under the Point Elliott treaty was the land that was exposed between high and low tide. The rest had been sold by the Bureau of Indian Affairs over the years to non-Indians, and only one tract of land that bordered the bay remained in Indians hands by 1968. You will recall that in late 1967 the Lummis were approached by representatives of a corporation that wanted to build a magnesium-oxide plant on Lummi Bay.

When news of the proposed plant was heard in Bellingham, Washington, people began to get concerned that the pollution from the process of reducing the ore to metal would ruin the fishing and recreation areas in Whatcom County. As this concern spread, a fortunate meeting occurred between Dr. Wallace Heath and some of the Lummis who were searching for an alternative use for the bay. Heath is a most remarkable person. Trained in desert ecology at the University of Arizona, he was at that time teaching at Western Washington State College in Bellingham and was very involved in developing natural and ecologically sound uses for lands and waters.

Heath worked as a volunteer in his spare time for one of Whatcom County's ecological groups in planning a county-wide program for the preservation of lands and waters. He visited the reservation and inquired why the Lummis were thinking of bringing the industry to their lands. The older and more traditional Lummis told him that they had been told there was no other use for such a freshwater bay. Heath knew a great deal about the old aquacultures of Hawaii, which the natives had built in those islands centuries before the coming of the white man, and he suggested that the Lummis think about developing an aquaculture.

The idea of systematically raising salmon, oysters, clams, and trout appealed tremendously to the traditional Lummis. They had always been fishermen and they wished to continue their traditions if at all possible. The next tribal meeting was flooded with the older people, who demanded that the idea of an aquaculture be given a chance. "After all," one of the elders said, "if it doesn't work we can always go ahead with the industry, but if the industry fails it will have ruined the waters forever and we can't do anything then." The tribe approved the idea of looking into the possibility of creating an aquaculture on Lummi Bay. They asked Dr. Heath to do some preliminary surveys on the bay to determine whether it would be feasible.

The State Oceanographic Commission gave the Lummis a grant of one thousand dollars to survey the aquatic life of the bay, and in the summer of 1968 Wally Heath and four Lummi teen-agers donned their diving suits and charted out the contours and marine life of Lummi Bay. By fall they had determined that the bay was an ideal place to build an aquaculture. The tidelands could be converted into a large pool with just the right depth to allow a number of fish to grow, and it appeared that oysters could flourish in the large pond that would be created. The tides could be channeled into the pond every day by a gate regulating the flow of water, so the Lummis would not even have to pump water back and forth to create circulation.

The Lummis had learned over the years to be extremely careful in revealing their plans to the Bureau of Indian Affairs or the local whites, and so they first sought a clarification of their legal rights to the bay. Fortunately the previous summer Congresswoman Julia Butler Hansen of Washington had asked the regional solicitor of the Bureau of Indian Affairs to clarify the rights of Indians to control the waters of their reservations, and he had stated that they owned the waters and could control them. The opinion had originally been written to clarify the status of the lands and waters of the Quinault reservation on the coast, but it applied to all the tribes of the Puget Sound area.

Since this legal opinion had already been widely circulated in the state, there was no way that the Bureau of Indian Affairs could deny that the Lummis owned the tidelands, and so they were free to go ahead with their plans. Dr. Heath had many acquaintances in the field of aquaculture, and they began to visit the reservation at his urging. Dr. Victor Loosanoof, professor of marine biology at the University of the Pacific and one of the world's foremost shellfish experts, came to the reservation and gave suggestions. Charles Black, a San Francisco businessman and husband of Shirley Temple, had developed a project at Pescadero Bay in California to grow oysters. His advice also aided the Lummis.

Through the Oceanic Foundation and Drs. Tim Joyner and Anthony Novotny, fisheries biologists of the Bureau of Commercial Fisheries were brought to meet the Lummis, and Taylor Pryor, president of the foundation, did everything he could to assist the Lummis in recruiting the best minds possible. The experts were quite impressed when they saw what Dr. Heath and the young Lummis had done: they already had a 1,000-foot-square grid chart laid out on the bay, and by using this chart they could determine the exact acreage and water level of every part of the bay. Having received encouragement from the experts to proceed, they packed their bags and headed to Washington, D.C., to see if they could get a grant from one of the federal agencies to build the project.

In February 1969 the Economic Development Administration gave the Lummis a grant of $143,220 to begin research and training on the aquaculture, and in June of that year the Indian Desk of the Office of Economic Opportunity gave the tribe a grant of three hundred thousand dollars to begin construction of a small oyster-, trout-, and salmon-raising pond, of 4.4 acres. Hopes for success ran high. The problem was that none of the Lummis had ever done anything of this magnitude before, and experts in pond construction had predicted that they would have all kinds of difficulties in getting the pond finished.

But no one had reckoned with the determination of the Lummis to build their pond. Experts said that the Lummis should plan to get fifty feet of dike built every day, and if they succeeded in meeting that rigorous schedule they could feel proud of themselves. But the Lummis were risking everything on this project, and so they all turned out to work on the pond. They did everything from operating the heavy equipment to grabbing shovels and moving the dirt by hand when necessary. Before anyone knew it, the Lummis were building one hundred feet of dike a day—an incredible rate, considering their tools.

The pond was dedicated with a galaxy of movie stars, senators, and congressmen in attendance and was followed by a salmon bake and plenty of other sea food. The people began immediately to raise oysters, and trout and salmon in their new pool. By this time most of the teen-agers had fallen in love with the project, and they began making new plans for their careers. Many went back to schools they had left in disgust several years earlier and started studying harder than they had ever studied to learn about shellfish in order to work in the project when it was finished. The tribe had a special aquaculture class, which taught all about the fish and oysters, and many older Indians who had dropped out of school years before enrolled in the classes. Everyone wanted to learn. I visited several of the classes, and some older Indians who knew little English could catch a fish and dissect it and name every part of the fish in Latin!

The original plans of the Lummis were to proceed very cautiously and build a 220-acre pond after they had shown that the 4.4-acre pond could successfully be used to raise fish. But the first results of the small pond were so outstanding that they decided to go ahead with a giant, 750-acre pond, which would put them into the commercial oyster and salmon market immediately. The 750-acre pond was a real challenge. It was one thing to close off less than five acres and raise several thousand salmon and oysters, but in a 750-acre pond they would be thinking in terms of hundreds of millions of salmon and oysters, and one change in temperature or sudden shift in the acidity of the water might destroy everything.

Another gigantic problem was simply building the pond. It was fairly easy to build a square pond of earth and rock dikes in the large bay, but building a 750-acre pond required closing most of the bay off. The tides were not bad on Lummi Bay, but as the dike was extended across the mouth of the bay, the area where the water could flow became narrower and narrower, and so the water rushed through this opening faster and faster. The dike would reach a point, after construction was nearly finished, when the tides would be so fast that they would carry away all the dirt that the people could place there in an eight-hour shift. At that point the Lummis would have to use the traditional method of closing a dike worked out centuries ago by the Dutch.

Even with all these problems apparent to them, the Lummis decided to go ahead with the larger pond, and in July 1970 the Economic Development Administration, impressed with what the tribe had accomplished already, granted them $1.5 million to build the large pond. The tribe began work immediately, very carefully using the grant to create additional jobs on the reservation. Since they needed gravel for the dike, they purchased a gravel-rich tract of 140 acres formerly belonging to the reservation, thereby cutting cost of materials. Nineteen Lummi men purchased gravel trucks of varying age and carried the gravel to the dike, avoiding the need for contracting the hauling job to a more expensive company.

In every way imaginable, the Lummis scrimped and saved,

because they realized that the cost of closing the dike would be so enormous that they would need every cent they had. To save money, many of the Lummis would come out to the dike in their odd hours and volunteer their time, after having worked a full day on their other jobs. Even grandmothers and grandfathers found ways to contribute to the job, if only by bringing sandwiches and hot coffee to the people working on the night shift. Sometimes they simply came out to the dike to encourage the workers and look with pride on the great dike that was slowly creeping its way across the mouth of the bay.

The dike, about three miles long, extended from Sandy Point around the major part of the bay to a point on the shore where the small pond had been built. By late fall 1970 the Lummis were averaging more than two hundred feet of dike per day. This construction involved hauling tons and tons of rock for a base to the dike and thousands of tons of sand and gravel to fill in between the rocks and finally thousands of tons of dirt for the top of the dike. The width of the dike was approximately sixteen feet at the top and ninety feet at the base, while its height was about sixteen feet. Building the large pond was unquestionably a tremendous undertaking.

The Lummis worked all through the winter, and when spring came, the rains, which fall almost continuously in the Pacific Northwest, increased, and hampered the work to a great extent. Yet whether it was rain or shine the determined Lummis kept working.

By late May they were ready to discuss closing the dike, and they called on a Dutch expert to advise them on how to do it. He flew over from Holland, carefully surveyed the dike, and suggested that the Lummis use the traditional method in view of the tides, which, since they were now confined to a small area, became very harsh and powerful. The traditional method of closing a dike was to build a large breakwater in front of the opening and allow the tides to crash on the breakwater while the people quickly filled in behind it. He told the tribe that it would cost about three hundred thousand dollars to close the dike—an amount the Lummis did not have.

Dave Hudson, one of the engineers who was helping to direct the project, came up with a novel idea that saved the day. He had Lummi aqualung divers pin a sheet of polyvinyl filter cloth over the bottom of the entrance to the bay. He figured that when the tide came rushing in, it would hit the plastic sheet and press it down on the floor of the bay instead of acting as a big scoop and digging the sand out. The sheet, when it was finally attached, covered an area of nine acres! Of course there were many smaller pieces, about the size of half a football field, fastened together to form this bigger sheet, but placing this much plastic flat in a rushing tide, forty feet below the surface of the water, was quite an accomplishment, especially when one considers that some of the Lummi aqualung divers were only teen-aged.

June 4, 1971, was chosen as the day to close the dike, and for weeks before the big event the Lummis worked night and day on the dike. They piled up gigantic piles of rock, sand, and gravel about a hundred yards from the edge so that on the day of closing they could simply move these monstrous piles with bulldozers into the opening. Every day, they saw the piles get larger and larger, but they realized that they had to close an opening some eight hundred feet wide in the deepest part of the bay without interruption.

Finally the great day came. Almost every member of the tribe turned out to work, from the smallest baby to the oldest grandparents. Twenty-seven dump trucks were brought to the dike, ready to charge to the gravel pit or to the place where they got their dirt. With ten giant earthmovers on the dike and several smaller bulldozers, the work was commenced. Working for thirty hours without stopping, the Lummis moved fifteen thousand cubic feet of rock, gravel, and earth into the opening in a frantic move to close the dike before it rained.

They finished, dead tired, seven hours before experts had predicted they would. The television stations had all been alerted to be at the dike at noon to film the closing of the dike. I was living in Bellingham at the time, and the Lummi leaders told me to be at the dike at noon to see the celebration. When we all got to the dike that morning, we were told that the Lummis had finished the closing at five and that everyone was at the picnic grounds celebrating. Not only had the Lummis finished the closing of the dike, but when I got out there at noon one could not tell where they had filled in, because they had not merely closed the gap but had finished the task completely, including grading the sides.

With the large pond now finished, the Lummis had to build a number of breeding ponds to raise the fingerlings in. The tribe built a large trout-breeding pond at the foot of the Cascades near their old friend Mt. Baker, where they could raise the trout to a respectable size before taking them in trucks down to the large pool. In the process of developing the trout hatchery and breeding pond, the Lummis discovered how to transform the trout from a freshwater fish to a salt-water fish. Using Donaldson trout as their test species, the Lummis showed that it is possible to get the trout accustomed to living in salt water in a matter of three weeks. When the Economic Development Administration learned that they had made such a discovery, it encouraged them to keep the process a trade secret of the tribe, and it remains so today.

In August 1972 the Lummis completed a large oyster hatchery built in the style of a traditional cedar longhouse. The hatchery is completely modern and is designed to produce 100 million seed oysters a year, making it the largest producer (in relation to the money invested) in the world. When the fish hatchery is placed together with the oyster operations, the Lummis are capable of producing 10 million fingerlings and 100 million oysters every year—a tremendous amount of seafood by anyone's standards.

Everything did not go as smoothly as one would imagine in the development of the aquaculture, however, and the dissension was in part due to the Bureau of Indian Affairs. They had tried a great many development schemes at Lummi, and in 1967, the very year the Lummis began thinking about the aquaculture program, the Bureau of Indian Affairs let it be known that they had "given up" on the Lummis and would no longer try to help them with development. The bureau had strongly supported the industrial development behind the scenes and was further angered by the refusal of the Lummis to approve the project.

As the aquaculture program expanded, the tribe needed to make various changes in its constitution and bylaws. A dissident group of Lummis, a handful of people who had supported the magnesium-oxide plant, wanted a provision written into the tribal constitution enabling them to launch recall petitions against individual tribal councilmen until they gained control of the council. The bureau saw this constitutional change as a way to get control of the tribe once again and insisted that the tribal rolls be brought up to date before a vote on the constitution could be held.

It had been traditional in the Pacific Northwest for the off-reservation people to oppose reservation developments on the theory that tribal funds should be divided on an individual basis, and the bureau thought that by making every Lummi eligible for membership in the tribe, eligible to vote on the constitution it could best support the group that was against the aquaculture. So bureau employees scurried around locating Lummis who had moved away from the reservation years before, and a campaign against the aquaculture began. But the tribal leaders were much more aware of Lummi opinion than the Bureau of Indian Affairs, and they took care to inform the off-reservation members of the opportunities that were being developed for all tribe members.

The off-reservation people were very impressed with the new aquaculture program, and many of them looked forward to the day when they could quit their jobs in the cities and return home to the reservation to work. When the vote on the constitution was finally held, the proaquaculture group swamped their opposition, the amendments to the tribal constitution were defeated, and the Bureau of Indian Affairs was left with a very embarrassed expression on its face. They had only succeeded in arousing a lot of interest, publicity, and support from off-reservation tribe members for the aquaculture project.

A much more dangerous group that fought the Lummis was the Lummi Bay Beach Association. It was made up of white property owners who owned lands along the beach. They had a great influence in the city of Bellingham and went to great lengths to criticize the aquaculture as a waste of money and a dangerous precedent in allowing uneducated Indians to "run things." Their first major attack was issued prior to a hearing held by the U. S. Army Corps of Engineers on the issuing of a license to the tribe to build the experimental pond.

Four petitions were sent to the Army listing various reasons why the project should not be built. The problem was that about fifty-nine people had signed the four petitions over and over again, averaging nearly four signatures apiece. On one petition five people signed three times each. They all accused the Lummis of trying to create a 2,200-acre pond that would harm wildlife and boating, although none could understand or explain how a pond designed to grow salmon, trout, and oysters scientifically could harm the wildlife.

Then a letter-writing campaign began that was truly incredible. Letters came from as far as Texas complaining about the aquaculture (although it was certain that the aquaculture would not affect property values in Texas). One letter writer accused the Lummis of deliberately placing oysters on the beach to cut the feet of trespassers, while others said that the project was a plot to cut off the wind. The chief accusation was that the fish would create a deadly smell that would stifle breathing.

When the hearing was actually held, the Lummi leaders took each and every complaint and patiently explained how the aquaculture would help improve rather than harm conditions. It was, of course, no contest, and the opposition made such fools of themselves that the Army had no choice but to approve the permit. One of the most vocal opponents of the project was a graduate student at the college who wrote many letters against both the project and the Lummi leaders. After the large pool was authorized and the tribe had a large training grant from the Office of Economic Opportunity, he demanded a job from the Lummis as a counselor!

One of the best things that happened to the Lummis was their meeting with Christopher Blake, a playwright and noted gourmet cook. The Lummis were in Washington, D.C., trying to get a grant, and they visited the National Press Club for lunch. They carried with them large posters illustrating the nature of their project, and since they had no place to put the posters while they ate, they simply propped them up in the lobby of the Press Club.

While visiting the club, Blake noticed the posters and asked where the Lummis were. They met over lunch, during which the Indians explained their project and their need for publicity in marketing their fish and oysters. Impressed, Blake returned home to New Orleans with a promise that the Lummis would send him samples of their products. Using these, he created several special new dishes and demonstrated them in the National Press Club and in an exclusive San Francisco restaurant.

With this very good publicity, the Lummis set about creating their own brand, which features a smiling Lummi on the label. They now ship and sell salmon and oysters all over the country. They have recently begun talks with Japanese businessmen about shipping sea foods to Japan under a special arrangement. Other tribes have copied the Lummis, and now several aquacultures are being planned by tribes of the area, and some inland tribes such as the Paiutes of Pyramid Lake, Nevada, are planning a freshwater-lake aquaculture.

Everyone is pleased that things have worked so well. And many people see a special providence in the aquaculture. When a tribe is reduced to owning only that land which is uncovered between high and low tides and still manages to turn that land into something very productive, it seems as though somebody up there is watching out for them.

chapter FIFTEEN

THE Pacific Northwest today is a scene of great activity. Not only are tribes beginning to recapture old cultural values and traditions, but the conflict between the Indians and the whites is at a fever pitch because of the struggle over fishing rights. In the past ten years, through the persistent efforts of such people as Hank Adams, the Indians have been able to present a fully documented story of their deprivation in the courts, and as judges have heard the amazing stories of federal and state oppression of Indians, court decisions have turned around to favor the tribes.

In 1970, as we have seen, the federal government was finally forced to sue the state of Washington because of the massive bad publicity coming out of the arrests at Tacoma. The case, known as *U.S.* v. *Washington*, dragged out for more than three years and was finally decided favorably for the Indians. The evidence was so overwhelming that even the judge, who began the case with an anti-Indian attitude, concluded that the Indians, under treaty, were entitled to half of the fish harvested in the waters of the state each year.

While the United States seemed to be supporting the tribes, it turned out that once again the Indians were being deprived of their rights by their federal trustees. Primarily through the hard work of Indian lobbyists, a sum of six hundred thousand dollars was appropriated by the Congress to assist the tribes in developing their own tribal rules and regulations for controlling fishing by Indians. But after the money had been appropriated, the tribes waited months for the Interior Department to consult with them about how the funds were to be allocated. They discovered that the Department of the Interior was stalling while trying to figure out a way to give the money to the Washington Fish and Game departments. Thus, once again, the victory of the tribes in the courts and Congress was being taken away from them by behind-the-scenes manipulations of the Interior Department.

It was not the first time in recent years that the Interior Department had blatantly violated federal laws. In the late 1940s the Bureau of Indian Affairs signed timber-cutting contracts on two gigantic tracts on the Quinault reservation. The Quinaults have the last good stand of western red cedar left on the coast, and with the lumber market in good condition and the quality of Quinault cedar so high, the larger trees are *each* worth between ten and fifteen thousand dollars.

Over the years, the Bureau of Indian Affairs has refused to police the manner in which the timber companies are cutting the timber. They have assigned one person to supervise the timber cutting; he arrives on the reservation in the middle of the morning and spends a leisurely day, returning to his office in time to go home at 4:30 P.M. Cutting of the timber begins at seven o'clock in the morning and often continues until dark. There is no accounting of the amount of timber cut in the hours when the bureau employee is not present or of what happens to the logs once they are cut. There is presently a lawsuit filed against the United States contending that the manner in which the bureau supervises the harvesting of Quinault timber leads to many practices that deprive Indians of a significant amount of income.

In 1970 the tribe began a new fish-hatchery program and was using the freshwater streams on the reservation as spawning places for the salmon. But the logging companies in their harvesting of timber destroyed a great many of the gravel beds necessary as spawning places. They had made it a practice to cut almost everything on the different tracts of forest land and were clear-cutting the Quinault lands, in direct violation of a federal law prohibiting clear-cutting of timber on an Indian reservation.

By the fall of 1971 things were clearly out of hand. The forest was being totally destroyed, and no replanting was being done even though the Bureau of Indian Affairs was collecting 10 per cent of the income from the timber for a reforestation program. And the salmon spawning beds were being rapidly destroyed by the giant machines used in cutting the timber. So the Quinaults blockaded the logging roads leading off the reservation, demanding that something be done about the situation. Two old cars were dragged across the narrow bridge connecting the timber lands and the state highway, and when the county police officials tried to serve a summons on the Quinaults, the vice-chairman of the tribe, Joe Delacruz, took an ax and chopped the summons in two.

The Interior Department, worried that things were becoming troublesome, promised to send out a special "task force" to discuss the problem. A selected group of bureaucrats arrived at the reservation and talked with Indians and lumber-company people alike. When the Quinaults pointed out the damage to their fishing program and the federal prohibition against clear-cutting their forest, they were told that the federal government only had a *moral* duty to preserve the forest, not a *legal* duty, even though it was clearly written in the Code of Federal Regulations that it was illegal to clear-cut Indian timber. In spite of the obvious liability that present practices seem to be creating, the Bureau of Indian Affairs has still not stopped the bad cutting practices, and the fish program remains in jeopardy because of the destruction of the spawning grounds. It seems as if only an act of God will be able to prevent the Bureau of Indian Affairs from supervising the final destruction of the Quinault reservation.

Activism seems so romantic: people visualize a heroic young Indian fighting the forces of destruction against almost impossible odds, always overcoming because his cause is right. But the Indians of the Pacific Northwest learned long ago that there is a great deal of danger and very little romance in their struggle. In January of 1971 Hank Adams and another Indian were checking the Nisqually fishing nets early one morning along the Nisqually River. While the other Indian walked along the riverbank, Hank fell asleep in the back of his car. Suddenly the door was opened, and as Hank raised his head sleepily a voice shouted, "This will teach you damn Indians."

A rifle barrel came into view, and as Hank tried to clear his head the rifle was fired point-blank at him. The bullet passed completely through his body and through the car door on the other side. Some white sportsmen had ambushed him! Hank was rushed to the hospital and, after emergency surgery, recovered. When he complained to the police about his near-fatal visitation from the two ambushers, the police called him a liar and demanded that he take a lie-detector test. They accused him of shooting himself in order to get publicity!

Hank refused to take a lie-detector test unless he was allowed to have an outside witness present who could testify to the results of the test. He figured that the police would simply change the results of the test and tell the newspapers, most of which were writing anti-Indian stories, that Hank had shot himself. When the police learned that they would have to have an outside witness observe the test, they refused to give it.

As far as can be determined, Hank Adams is the only Indian who has been ambushed by sportsmen because of the fishing-rights struggle. But there have been other incidents nearly as disturbing. In 1973 the Washington National Guard, while on summer maneuvers at Fort Lewis, used the Nisquallies as their theoretical enemy, and war games were played that involved an invasion and extermination of the Nisqually tribe. When the Indians discovered that they were the subjects of the summer frolic, they protested to state officials, who gave a very lame excuse about Indians being too sensitive. Later the Nisquallies discovered that the Department of Game was keeping files on their personal lives to determine how they could best control the Nisquallies.

The fishing-rights struggle will probably continue for the rest of the century or as long as the Indians have the strength to continue it. Considering that most of the tribes have been fishing for centuries in the same places they are fishing today, it seems unlikely that they will abandon their traditional life within the foreseeable future. The pity is that the odds are so heavily against the Indians. Whites, particularly sportsmen, blame the decline of fish on the Indians and completely overlook the effects of the great power-generating dams and the many heavy industries that pollute the river. Even the public doesn't seem to realize that there are so few Indians who actually do fish that even if they were to fish day and night all year long they would not make much impact on the total number of fish.

In 1974, under the new decision of Judge Boldt, which allowed the Indians to catch their share of the fish, state officials went out of their way to juggle the figures of fish catches in an effort to show that Indian fishing was destroying the catch. The catch of fish seemed to be greatly declining as a result of Indian fishing, and Governor Dan Evans asked President Ford to declare the salmon industry a "major disaster area," apparently in an effort to gain a favorable political image among sportsmen. Everyone was busy accusing the Indians of ruining the fishing industry until Mike Moyer, the director of planning for the Swinomish tribe, began to recite hard facts and figures about the 1974 catch.

The total Indian catch in 1974 was up 5 per cent from the previous year, but the total was still only 12 per cent of the total number of fish caught in the state. The reason why there had been such bad fishing was that the number of days allowed to fishermen had been reduced. But in spite of the reduction in the number of days on which whites were allowed to fish, 1974 was the second-greatest year on record for the salmon industry. State departments in charge of selling fishing licenses had deliberately oversold the number of licenses so that each fisherman would feel that he was being deprived of his livelihood because of the lower number of fishing days allowed.

In 1974 the purse-seine licenses increased from 330 to 437, a thirty-two per cent increase. Gill-net licenses increased from 1,303 to 1,988, a fifty-three per cent increase. Moyer pointed out that in the Skagit River alone fifteen thousand coho salmon were allowed to escape capture and return up the river to spawn instead of the usual five thousand. So from every angle except superficial statistics, 1974 was a good year for fishing, particularly for the salmon industry, and there were a record number of fish allowed to return to their spawning grounds.

By bringing out statistics the Indians were able to show that, far from ruining the salmon industry, they were hardly catching many more than they had always caught but that the state officials had ensured that many more fishermen than usual would fish fewer days than usual and would return home from their fishing discontented and mad at the Indians. The fishing-rights struggle seems to be one in which Indians continuously have to fight not only state and federal officials who are violating federal laws but the people who figure statistics, to prevent them from creating an artificial situation in which no one is ever sure what the facts are.

Since about 1967, the smaller tribes in the Puget Sound area have organized a group called "Small Tribes of Western Washington," or STOWW, to present their case before the government and the public. The founding president, Roy George, a Nooksack, built a strong, politically active organization that exerted great influence among the Indian tribes of the country, and his successor, Leo LeClair, a Muckleshoot, has concentrated on the development of good programs that are designed to serve the many small Indian communities in the area. While STOWW has concentrated so far on political organization and program development, there is every indication that economic development programs built on the fishing rights of the different tribes will eventually bring all the tribes together.

From a widely scattered grouping of villages to the modern organizations of today, the Indians of the Pacific Northwest have made great political strides in learning how to come together for a common purpose. While some parts of their old culture have vanished, they have discovered new things to replace them, and with the Lummis and the Quinaults taking the lead in the development of aquacultures, the future shows a much greater promise than the past has delivered.

As the other tribes finally develop their fishing resources, there are plans to create a regional Indian label for sale of canned fish products, and one day you may be in the neighborhood supermarket and see a smiling Indian on the label of a can of salmon. You will know from his smile that things are still pretty exciting in the Pacific Northwest.

INDEX

Vine Deloria, Jr., was born on the Pine Ridge Indian Reservation in South Dakota. He became familiar with the Indians of the Pacific Northwest during the three years he served as executive director of the National Congress of American Indians and while living in Bellingham, Washington, and working with the Lummi and other tribes on legal problems. He has also served as chairman of the Institute for the Development of Indian Law and appeared as an expert witness on the legal problems of Indians at the Wounded Knee trials.

Mr. Deloria is the author of several books about the American Indians and their heritage, including the best-selling *Custer Died for Your Sins*.